MEMOIR OF A

Jewish American Christian

JEFFREY LUDWIG

ISBN: 1482671875
ISBN-13: 9781482671872

This book is dedicated to my devoted wife,
Zenaida Ludwig, to my daughter,
Hannah Ludwig, and to my friend
Pastor Doug VanderMeulen.

CONTENTS

FORWARD

God, through the voice of His son, Jesus Christ, is calling every man, woman, and child on the face of the Earth to believe in Him. He is especially calling the Jewish people, my brothers and sisters, the chosen ones of the House of Israel. You see, Jesus told his disciples that a prophet is [often] not recognized in his own land after he, Jesus, had failed to heal all but a few in the Galilee district where he was born and raised. Yet, at the same time, he promised that his followers would do all that he did and even greater things. It seems to me that successfully bringing the gospel to the Jewish people is one of those "greater things." Only a relatively small number of the Jewish people accepted and followed Jesus, although, owing to his charisma and great teaching and healing powers, multitudes trailed after him desiring to hear him speak and to watch him perform miracles. Those multitudes, we might say, were classic "hearers of the Word" who were not doers. The doers followed Jesus, witnessed his ascension, and were present to receive the outpouring of the Holy Spirit in the Upper Room on the day of Pentecost.

Recently a friend of mine said, "Nobody wants to be a Jew except the Jews." He is himself Jewish, and together we had a good laugh over the deep truth of that comment. Paul wrote that the belief of the gentiles was intended by God to provoke the Jews to envy, and, because of that envy, finally to convert their souls of unbelief to souls of belief. Yet, over the centuries, the reaction of the Jewish community has not been one of envy. Rather, it has been one of rejection of Jesus' messiahship, perennial withdrawal into Talmudic hairsplitting, as well as despair and hatred in reaction to persecutions and ostracism by the larger gentile/Christian communities (often done in the name of Jesus Christ). The Jewish community has largely been perplexed, suspicious, defiant, or openly hostile to Christian attempts to spread the gospel to it. Often the preaching of the gospel was accompanied by force, and this meant that the acceptance of the gospel, instead of being a source of joy and hope, was a source of humiliation as well as spiritual and physical degradation in a hostile world.

This memoir is an attempt to cut through the centuries old horror that Jews feel at the mention of Christianity and of Jesus Christ. It is a kind of interpretive memoir where I look back at my life as a relatively assimilated American Jew, and refract my experiences through the lens of my relationship with the living God, Jesus Christ, also called Yeshua Hamaschiach in the Hebrew. It is an attempt to touch the Jewish heart, so that my fellow Jews can

be at once amused and feel understood. The Jewish
world that I have known is one filled with brilliance
and wit, yet at the same time with great anxieties and
longings, charm and *joi de vivre* alongside a deep
sense of disappointment and failure. The Jewish
personality can be at once warm and hostile, open,
yet suddenly withdrawn and dark.

Nothing I have read recently has captured a real
sense of the mainstream American Jewish personality
of the second half of the twentieth century. Some
writers have drawn close to an accurate portrayal;
yet I find an absence of spiritual perspective. What
hope is there for the Jew? How are we to understand
various obsessions or painful thoughts of the Jewish
community? Are we simply to be amused and
"accepting," or are we to see if there is a way out?
Unequivocally, I believe there is a way out of the
dilemmas that face the Jewish person as he or she
faces a world often filled with painful circumstances.

Chapter One:

Songs of Childhood

We begin with three names; Giselle McKenzie, Dorothy Collins, and Snooky Lanson. Every Saturday night for years as a child, I watched these singers on "Your Hit Parade," a Saturday night TV show dedicated to performing the top musical hits in America during that week. From Saturday to Saturday, I would hypnotize myself by singing phrases of the songs over and over again to myself, allowing my spirit to get drawn into the sentimental and romantic flow of the lyrics, and watering a garden of romantic fantasy where I, as a handsome crooner, woo and win millions of ladies, and live out my life in a pop tune euphoria. Over and over the refrain, "Take my hand, I'm a stranger in paradise...." would waft as a balmy and sensuous breeze through the open chambers of my mind. I would remember Snooky costumed as a sultan, with a turban on his head, crooning to some lovely harem girls, "...all lost in a wonderland...a stranger no mo-o-ore...." And Giselle and Dorothy, so lively, cheerful, and womanly! "Why can't my mother be like them," I would ask myself. Will women like that be in my future? I already know the lyrics they love. Will I be found worthy?

Through the same years of my youth, Shirley, who lived in the row house next door, would constantly practice her favorite song on the piano. Like a magic musical suggestion, as soon as she began playing the melody, as soon as the notes came through the walls of the row house, or through the open windows in the summertime, the lyrics would begin spinning through my mind, "I'm wild again, beguiled again, a whimpering simpering child again, bewitched, bothered, and bewildered am I…am I…." (We all loved Nat King Cole!) Shirley and I and millions of others were in the same trance. We were just like the people of Babylonia. First the sweet music played, and then we were all to bow down to the golden image of the king. We worshipped ourselves and the world, the USA in the late nineteen forties and early fifties. What could be more beautiful?...

And what about Vaughn Monroe? "An old cowpoke went ridin' out one dark and windy day… Upon a windy ridge he rested as he went along his way…when all at once he chanced to see a ridin' in the sky, the devil's herd of cattle there…a ridin' up so high… Yippee aye yo-o-o, yippee aye aaay…the ghost riders in the s-k-y…." I liked the eerie, shadowy images the words evoked. I liked feeling manly like the cowboy alone with supernatural danger. And Vaughn's deep voice held out the hope that someday I would speak and sing basso profundo, a man among men.

So many songs floated through my mind day after day, year after year: "Mr. Sandman, send me a dream, make her the cutest that I've ever seen; give her two lips like roses in clover, then tell me that my lonesome nights are over. Sandman, I'm all alone, send me somebody to call my own. Puhleeze send down your magic beam…Mr. Sandman send me a dream." Maybe Giselle or Dorothy would appear magically to hug me and kiss me and stay with me forever?

I would be doing my homework, or sitting through one of Mrs. DiIoia's geography lessons, or playing checkers with Barry, when suddenly words would come… "You don't need analyzin', it's not so surprizin', you feel very strange indeed…Your heart goes pitter-patter, I know just what's the matter 'cause I've been there once or twice…you're not sick, you're just in love…." That's right Jeff, an inner prompting would tell my brain, you don't need analyzing. You're not sick (YOU'RE NOT, YOU'RE NOT!!). Just keep smiling. Just keep doing your homework. Just keep playing checkers and monopoly. Just keep working up a sweat playing stickball. You're not sick, you're just in love. Yes. That must be it. Sleepless nights, bad dreams, heart palpitations. I'm not sick. It must be….but, but,…I, I…don't love ANYBODY!! No. No. that's not true. I love Dad. I really love Dad. I would do anything for Dad. Dad. Dad. I ree-all-ly love you. What about Mom? Mom? I want to love her. I should love her. She's my mother. Mom, I L—; Mom, I LO–; Mom, I LOV-;…Mom, I HATE YOU, I HATE YOU WITH A PASSION. I HATE YOU!!!

Yes indeed. I was sick. I was sick with sin and vain imaginings. The songs of childhood were my daydreams of love and power. In them and through them, I felt a buoyancy and a pseudo-hopefulness. The songs vibrated with unreality. My spirit was awash with sentimentality. It seemed that my dream of love came through the sounds of the airwaves and the video waves projected electronically into my being.

The love I imagined, the love I expected, the love I hoped for was not REAL love, for REAL love is found in the heart. Real love is spiritual. Real love is the enthroned and very real presence of Yeshua Hamaschiach, the Son of God who was born one chilly morning two thousand years ago.

"God so loved the world that he gave his only begotten son that whosoever believes in him will not perish by will have everlasting life." (John 3:16) The reality of God's love was unknown to me growing up. I had not even heard of it; yet, even in my being I sensed the inadequacy of the love ghosts of the hit parade. You see, for all the melodies of love, for all the fantasies, for all the false promises onTV and radio about the wondrous satisfactions of romantic love, and Marlboro man adulthood, it became clear to me that I did not love my mother. This great personal reality impressed itself on my whole personality all my days, and, eventually, on my conscious mind.

You see, nothing in this world could point the way for me to love my mother; yet my sense of guilt over the hate I felt for her, and my sense of the injustice of my reactions to her, tormented me all my days until the Lord God of all creation took full control of my heart and mind.

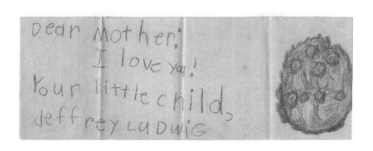

Mother's Day Card Kindergarten

JLAge 5, With Father and Mother.

No matter how much I consciously accepted my desire to be free of my mother, and my so-called negative feelings and attitudes towards her, the unconscious weight of my guilt, my attachment to her, my need to have her accept my resentment and rejection, my desire to change my mother into the woman of fantasy whom I longed for her to be, all combined to pull me back towards her, to unsettle my mental balance (to keep that balance from balancing), and to prove to me that under the Jewish mother jokes was an inescapable nightmare that needed to be (re)solved.

You see, I didn't love my mother, and I could not sing my way out of it, I could not study my way out of it, I could not party my way out of it, and later as a writer, I could not write my way out of it. Creativity wasn't the answer, nor scholarship, nor was success, nor was failure, nor was drinking, nor were a thousand diversions and a million trillion speculations and bursts of intellectual vigor. The fact remains that the hate of my life, the poison of hating the person I was "supposed" to love the most could only be counteracted by the love of my life. That love, like the peace He gives, passes all understanding. This love is like a radioisotope. It has particles that continue to radiate their power for thousands of years. The particles of love "radioactivity," so to speak, destroy or burn up the material of hate.

Belle Ludwig in her 50's; Ellis Ludwig in his 20's;
Belle with her younger brother and mother

John the Baptist said that he baptized with
water, but one would follow who would baptize
with fire. Yeshua, Jesus, was that one. The fire is
the power of infinite mercy and love, forgiveness

and hope. Yes, dear reader, the Jews 2000 years ago knew something about repentance. They came in great numbers to be baptized by John in the wilderness, and to repent of their sins awaiting the great advent of the Messiah. Messiah also cried out for repentance, "Repent ye, repent ye, for the Kingdom of Heaven is at hand," he said. Yet, at the same time, he was "the way, the truth, and the life." In being the way, the "strait gate" and "narrow way" unto eternal life, he thus takes us far beyond our initial repentance. Thus, to repent in Christ is different from repenting under the law, and is rightly called the "new birth." This repentance is not only repentance for our sins, but acceptance of Yeshua, Jesus Christ, as our Messiah, our Savior, Our Lord. We are asked to confess with our mouths that Jesus is Lord, and believe with our hearts that he rose from the dead. This puts a stamp of love, and a stamp of eternal life, on our repentance which simply saying "I'm sorry" to God in a general sense will never do. None comes to the Father except through the Son. Thus, it is only through Yeshua that we are saved, only through that name and His reality do we become heirs of the Messianic promises of the Old Testament ("tanakh").

The hit parade of hit songs goes on although Snooky, Giselle, and Dorothy are long gone. Yet, the dreams of love, and the bewitched, bothered, and bewildered melancholy have left me. I am no longer in a trance. I am no longer seeing ghosts and imaginary partners who will lift away my pain, or carry me off to the land of Nod through some erotic ether. I no longer hate my mother. I love my mother.

God came to me. He chose me and calls me His own. He consoles me even now. He is my Comforter. He has moved me from the lifeless altar of daydreams to unchanging and acceptable (to God) practices of prayer, praise, and worship. I am removed by Jesus from domination by false values to true spirituality, from *theoria* about God to *praxis*, from corruption to the path of perfection, from regrets, malaise, and guilt to secure hope in the life to come.

"Holy, holy, holy, Lord God Almighty, early in the morning, my song shall rise to thee." Thank you almighty God, thank you son of God, thank you Holy Spirit ("ruach kadosh") for blessing my life today. May the reader of this book be likewise blessed, and make the breakthrough to true repentance for sins and an eternal relationship with Yeshua Hamaschiach.

Chapter Two:

Once Upon a Time in Southwest Philadelphia

Fifty years ago I left Philadelphia. For twenty years I lived on Beaumont Street. It is a classic, narrow, Philadelphia street, with about twenty row houses on each side. Each house had its front lawn sloping down from a cozy porch. At the top of the lawn in front of our house was a small patch of garden where my mother grew her precious purple irises that bloomed twice every season, and then wilted into oblivion. Our second story was painted white with green trim. The floor of the porch was made of wooden slats painted gray, fronted by a railing with white spokes and a green handrail. And every house on the block had a garage in the back under the dining room, accessed via a driveway that ran the length of the block along the back of the houses.

I remember walking down the street, and can still remember every crack demarcating each square of cement sidewalk. Toby, the cop's daughter, told me I could not pass the line of the cement in front of her house. She dared me to cross the line. When I crossed the line, she hit me. I cried. I was ashamed that I was afraid of a girl.

I liked to walk to 59th and Warrington, and cross the triangle where there was a gas station (is it still there today?) that stood between the houses and the park. After crossing, one entered Cobbs Creek Park. There I could walk down the slope to a narrow dirt path that extended the length of the park alongside a shallow creek.

Skimming stones across the creek was something I liked to do as a boy. You had to find the right kind of flat stones to get a really good skim. Good skims were determined by the number of plip-plops across the shallow water. At another point on the creek there were larger wet stones that formed a slippery foot bridge across the creek. It was clear to me that I would not drown if my foot slipped off the bridge; yet, I still dreaded the thought of slipping in even up to my shins. Despite my fear, venturing across the footbridge I never fell in. On the other side you climbed up a little hill and were in a cemetery. The cemetery was a most quiet neighborhood (ha-ha); however I do not recall feeling either morbidly curious or afraid, though I am certain I would not have gone there at night.

If I did not walk across the stony foot bridge, but continued to follow the path, I would come to the public tennis courts. These were wonderful asphalt courts. My father and older brother would play there, and once I was ten years old, I would enjoy many hours with my friends playing tennis. It was fun climbing up the hill from the tennis courts and walking at street level alongside Cobbs Creek

Parkway up to where it would turn towards 58th and Baltimore Avenue and the site of the public library.

I was acutely aware that I was near the city limits at that point. I sensed that I was near a strange territory that could only be vaguely understood as OUTSIDE PHILADELPHIA. At 61st & Baltimore, the subway surface car line ended, and I knew that Rte. 1 began. I was not sure where Rte. 1 went. If someone had asked me, I would have said, "It goes out towards Lancaster. That's the road to take if you want to see the Pennsylvania Dutch." Where were the Pennsylvania Dutch? I had no idea, but was intrigued by the thought that they rejected the wearing of zippers. To this day I do not know if that is true or where Rte. 1 leads. There are bus tours from downtown Brooklyn where I now live, but when the people come back they talk mostly about the great apple pies of the Pennsylvania Dutch. I never ask about the zippers or Rte. 1.

When I was a little boy, the #46 trolley car ran along 58th Street on tracks. The #46 was powered by electricity from an overhead wire that was connected to each car by a pole extended from the roof of the car to the wire. The trolley car was shaped like a raised rectangular box. The car was not operated by pedals and a steering wheel, but by using handles. The cars were two man cars manned by a motorman and a conductor. In that era, people could be trusted to walk to the middle of the car to pay their fares.

My father worked for the Philadelphia Transit Authority (now Septa), and I would love to ride the #46 when he would be either the motorman or conductor. I was so proud to be related to this public figure. If he were in charge of this big car, with all these people, he must be a personage, a great man. That's my father! How I beamed!

Belle & Ellis 1960 (Jeffrey was 19)

My grade school, Longstreth, was at 58th and Windsor. It was a safe harbor. My friends went there, my cousin went there, and I learned all the basics I would need for the REST OF MY LIFE. My teachers were Miss Invernisi, Mrs. Rothenberg, Miss Claybaugh, Miss Dunn (she wore big hats and put on operettas), Miss Kilburn, Miss Blalock (my cousin tells me she became principal), and Mrs. DiIoia (she gave tons of homework). I loved to talk and play board games with Ricky Rake and Sammy Liebman. I competed for grades with Neil Tannenbaum, Hoyt Hobbs, and Bob Evans. I deeply loved Eva Rangnow, and hoped either that my parents would adopt her or that someday we would marry. I was also fascinated, though in a less pure way, with Annette Cohen and Lucia Aleeva. Some kids said I had a big nose. Others said I had a nice smile (wasn't that Eva?). Steve Himmelstein and Bobbie Starks were also in my class. They were tough kids, not like me. But I was proud to know them. I felt I was tougher just because I was friends with them. Joan Teacher was a friend too, along with Louis and Marie.

6th Grade Report Card

If you walked down Warrington to 54th, you arrived at Shaw Junior High. That is where I attended school after graduating from Longstreth. There was a candy store across from Shaw where the bad boys hung out and smoked. I passed them, half-scornful yet half-wishing I were Italian and tough so I could join in.

Shaw was a monstrosity. Students pushed teachers in the lunchroom. There were food fights. Gangs roved the yard at lunchtime, and would hang certain students by their belts from the spiked school fence. The school disciplinarian and hero was Mr. Roeser, who was a gym teacher. He also refereed events at the Penn Relays. "Don't mess with Mr. Roeser," was the understanding. Once in gym class, he took the pants off a defiant boy. Students said he slapped his rear end also, but I didn't see that. It was great to see the punk humiliated. Mr. Roeser was the man for the job.

At Shaw, students would shakedown other students (a far cry from Miss Dunn's operettas!).

At Shaw I met kids from other neighborhoods. Some of the real tough ones were also smart. I learned that you can't tell a book by its cover. Kids started talking about sex. There was "experimentation" in the school yard and the hallways.

Springfield Avenue was a block over from Warrington. Gloria lived on Springfield. She was my girlfriend for about three weeks when I was thirteen.

One block past Springfield is Chester Avenue. There I boarded the #13 subway surface line (an electric trolley with a streamlined bullet-like shape) every morning for three years on my way to Central High School. Central is located in the north central part of the city in an area known as Olney. To get there, I would need to transfer to the Broad Street Subway and travel to the end of the line, and then walk three blocks.

When I enrolled in this high school, I left my neighborhood. It was really good to get away from Shaw. I hated the violence and turmoil of that setting where I spent three miserable years. The main light for me was that when I anticipated going to Central in 10th grade, my French teacher told me that at that great high school they studied fourteen conjugations of French in 9th grade whereas at Shaw, only six were taught. Then, without charge, she volunteered to teach me the other eight conjugations after school so that I would not be behind when I arrived at Central. What a kind and wonderful giver that woman was! In fact, when I began at Central, French was my best subject.

As I waited for the #13 one day on my way to high school, Joe Terranova, one of the Italian toughs from Shaw, waved to me from a red Thunderbird. He had joined a rock group, Danny and the Juniors, and had become a celebrity. I saw him on the Patti Page show. Yes, I was glad to get away from Shaw, but on the other hand, it was nice to know a celebrity.

The big school on the hill at Ogontz and Olney Avenues (Central High) was the beginning of a different chapter in my life. Goodbye 58th Street.

Goodbye Longstreth and Shaw. Goodbye Warrington and Florence and Springfield Aves. Something bigger and better was in store for me....

Chapter Three :

A Spoiled Brat

'Honor thy Father and Thy Mother' did not exist in my heart as a child. My love for my father was a morbid idealization and fascination. I wanted to grow up to be a boaster, a smart-aleck, and a leader as I supposed him to be. My love for my father was not based on knowledge or insight into his personality. I had no desire to be kind to him, nor any sense of duty. My admiration was based on fear. His boasts about beating people up penetrated deeply into my mind. I leaned on him, but at the same time felt cowed, intimidated. He was there to protect me. But what if I stepped out of line? What then? What if I went on my own? What if I opposed him?

How guilty and afraid I felt when, on one occasion, he asked me to get him a pack of cigarettes in another room, and I refused. Then, later, I asked him something, and he said, "figure it out yourself," or "get it yourself…." as retaliation for my earlier refusal. I felt very ashamed. How could I have been so foolish as not to get him the cigarettes? Would he withdraw his love? Would I have to go it alone in a friendless world?

At one time, my father and I were playing gin rummy. I had lost again, perhaps the thirteenth game in a row. I remember asking my father, "Why is it that even though you taught me how to play gin rummy, and I apply all the 'tricks' you taught me, I never win when I play you?" My father answered with a broad smirking smile on his face, "I taught you, but I didn't teach you EVERYTHING I know." This answer surprised me, and I sensed the full significance of this for my life. Yet, I did not rebel. This response was rationalized by me. Instead of perceiving this remark as the put down of a manipulative mind, I called it "wisdom." "How smart of my father," I thought, "surely I must remember to do the same thing in life, for surely it is the formula for staying on top." Yes, it was clear to me. Only a sucker would teach his son how to play cards well enough to beat him. My obedience to my father was based more on fear than on love, and the love I felt was a love based on the bad tendency of the mind ("*yetzer harah*") rather than on the good tendency of mind ("*yetzer hatov*").

Nothing my mother said or did pleased me. I criticized her cooking; I ridiculed her afternoon naps; I found her footsteps to be too heavy, her laughter too frivolous, her speech irritating, etc. To me, her eyes looked dead; she was too fat; her comments on the relatives were tedious. I do not remember having any good thoughts about my mother. Only twenty years after I left home do I recall finding any good memories about her, more out of desire to be fair-minded than out of genuine love and appreciation. If you do not know it already, dear reader, our hearts need to respond to others in sincere and genuine love and appreciation, and not just a facsimile to be called "looking concerned." Seeming to care will not cut it with God.

Complaining about her and disliking her were habits.

"Mom, why do you embarrass me like this in front of my friends?" I asked. My mother had brought me chocolate milk at morning recess, and called me over to the fence of the schoolyard to give it to me.

"I don't see why you mind, Jeffrey," she said. "You don't eat a good breakfast, and a growing boy has to have something during the morning. It's too long to go until lunch without eating anything."

"You're overprotective. You worry about me too much. Do the other kids' mothers bring them milk? Look! You're the only one here. Doesn't that make you think?!"

"No. Now drink the milk. The other kids probably have a good breakfast, and maybe their mothers don't CARE. But I do."

"Care? You're the one who doesn't care. I wish I never had a   mother like you. All you do is make trouble for me. Why don't you listen to me instead of telling me how much you care?! I wish I never was born. I wish you weren't my mother!"

Shouting with a raging spirit were my habits in dealing with my mother, and she in turn would be raging at me. I don't remember whose raging started first. On the other hand, my father could put me down, insult me, cheat me out of victory in card games, point out my faults, and I would just smile and be agreeable. With my mother, literally any little something would send me into a cursing, raging tantrum. Woe is the unruly child! Woe is the child who is not ministered to with serious discipline and grave spiritual counsel. If the meek shall inherit the earth (as they most certainly will), then truly I was the all-time loser!

Jeffrey Ludwig was arrogant and despicably insubordinate towards his mother. I was angry, challenging, defiant, disobedient and anarchistic. Instead of being grateful for the milk, and not giving the matter a second thought, I fumed and fretted. Where was love? Where was gratitude? Where was appreciation? Where was counting my blessings?

My father, I believed, enjoyed the spectacle of my mother's helplessness and frustration in dealing with me. He never punished me for back-talking my mother, nor for yelling at her, nor, once, for striking her (God have mercy upon me!). Yet, surely had I spoken to him as I had spoken to her, I would have been pulverized. All he would say to me was "mom really loves you." Perhaps he took a sadistic delight in seeing my mother tortured and abused. Did he consider her feelings as he ran from skirt to skirt in a never-ending battle to prove his manhood? Did he consider the family when he frittered away money at the racetrack or gambling at card games and checkers? Although, it should be stated that we never experienced want – the basic needs of life were always met, and money was saved for my college education.

Where was his integrity? We are told by Our Lord and Savior to love thy neighbor as thyself. Yet, the unloving soul will gloat about his neighbor's (wife's) misfortunes provided he is not likewise struck. As long as he did not lose at gin rummy, as long as did not have to suffer the tantrums and cursing attacks, as long as he didn't have to stay home and listen to my *noodnik* ways ("Mom, I'm so bored...what should I do?....) day after day insatiably looking for attention, craving a love which only God Almighty can give.

My father never called me to account for my behavior. In his presence, I was an incorrigible sycophant. That was what he desired. As long as his ego was flattered, and his desire for power appeased, he could not care less what happened in his absence.

"Ellis, this boy was terrible today; I'm beside myself; I don't know what to do with him," my mother cried out to my father as he came through the door at the end of his day's work. I was seated on the couch and looked up at him. We had been through this scene many times.

"What did he do this time?" my father asked, with his lips tightly drawn and his square jaw hard, set and jutting out even more than usual.

"He cursed me, that's what he did!" my mother screamed. "I told him he couldn't go out to play – it's going to rain any minute, and I don't want him getting soaked and getting a chill.... And do you know what he said to his MOTHER?... He said, 'I hate you. I hate this house. I hate your guts...You're a dirty rotten —.' Then he wouldn't drink his juice, and he's been stomping around. Then he went up to his room and slammed his door shut, and I had to yell at him for a half-hour before he came out and came back downstairs...."

My father looked at me sternly. I didn't say anything. "Don't worry," my father said, "this kid is gonna learn that he can't act that way and he can't talk that way."

He started to unbuckle his belt and drew the belt through the loops in his pants. By this time, he was standing between my mother and me, facing me, and was looping the belt. As he stretched the belt out to make sure he had plenty of tension, he gave me a wink. "Now I'm going to beat the heck out of this kid so he never forgets to act right."

Dad & Mom, 2ⁿᵈ and 3ʳᵈ on right; Across from two of Dad's brothers and their wives; Dad's brother-in-law is on his left.

At these words, my mother suddenly had a change of heart. "Beat him?! Ellis! No! Don't hurt him. He's bad, but don't beat him. Please don't beat him! Make him apologize. Make him say he's sorry, but don't beat him. Please Ellis! Please!"

My father paused a second, and then began slipping his belt back through the loops of his pants. "All right, Belle, for your sake I won't beat him this time (he winked at me again), but he had better apologize. Jeff, I want you to apologize to your mother this minute."

"O.K.Dad," I replied. "Mom, I'm sorry that I said the things that I said, and I'm sorry that I didn't come down from my room sooner. But you see I was right about going outside. It didn't rain, and I could have gone out to play, and I wouldn't have gotten wet."

Do you think my father was clever and humorous to have winked? Do you think my father was right to mock my mother by playing through this scenario? Do you consider my father a wise, permissive parent? Or do you see in him a cunning and unscrupulous parent who failed to walk on "paths of righteousness for His Name's sake?" Was his so-called tolerance righteous, or was it a failure of parental duty?

Consider dear reader the basic and eternally true commandment to HONOR THY FATHER AND THY MOTHER. Was my behavior dishonoring my mother? And does not the Word of God say that a man shall leave his mother and his father and cleave to his wife as one flesh. And therefore, dear reader, would it not be true to say that in dishonoring my mother with curses, abusive rages, and outright disobedience that I was also dishonoring my father? If they were married in one flesh, then surely such behavior indicates to me that they were divorced in spirit. Unable to agree on the raising of a child in spirit and in truth, my mother turned in frustration and helplessness for help to the very individual who was committed to sabotaging her efforts, separating himself from her legitimate desire for respect, and who, as a father, is a mere poseur who selfishly desired to save his own skin while, at the same time, appearing to be a wise judge, mediator, and household executive.

Yes, now is the time to look at your own lives. What rationalizations are driving you away from your parental duties? Are you disciplining your children? Are you standing together with your husband or wife? Is your life as a family disciplined by prayer and a walk with God governed by a sober, sincere, and altogether righteous understanding of the difference between right and wrong? Have you followed the "highway in the wilderness" described by Isaiah or have you been floundering in an abyss of frustration and permissive indolence, searching, so to speak, not for a highway on which to travel straight and speedily towards God Almighty, but for a picnic ground where you may have a more casual relationship with the Almighty?

Woe on the conflicted family life of this land: How much of this rottenness of life, the disintegration of industry, and of the family, can be traced to the wisecracking, back-talking, angry retaliation of children against one or both of their parents?

How much pain in my psyche as an adult was brought on by my years of disobedience towards my mother in childhood and how much of that disobedience was the result of a perfidious collusion between my father and me whereby I would treat him as my idol, to be feared and worshipped, and he would traitorously support me in my power struggle with my mother? And then, when one considers the pain that this spoiled brat brought into the lives of many others through his troublemaking ways decade after decade, then it seems that the magnitude of this dishonor and disobedience, was and is most grievous.

What about my apology to my mother? It was not sufficient! It was verbal and a technique not unlike my father's threat and subsequent wink. What was the technique intended to do? It was intended to create the illusion of repentance. It was not sincere and from the heart, but a mere strategy. It was a word that did not arise from love or truth, but from the manipulative lying spirit ruled by the enemy.

Yet, the sense of power that grew as I won victory after victory over my mother, with my father's help, reached a pitch where I began to test it on my father. My unruliness began breaking out in new directions. I began losing a sense of fear of my father, and my unbounded sense of power (omnipotence fantasies) began to break out more and more frequently.

"Why can't I have the book?" I shouted at my father.

"Because it's too expensive," he answered.

"I never can have anything I want," I cried. "All you ever say is 'It's too expensive' or 'We can't afford it'. Why can't I have things like the other kids?!"

"Jeff," he replied with the usual smirk on his face, "you have all kinds of things that the other kids have, and lots of things they don't have – games, an erector set, lots of things."

"Well, I'm fed up," I replied. I went upstairs and threw socks, underwear, a shirt and a pair of pants in a brown paper bag, and marched downstairs.

"I'm leaving home," I declared.

My father, still smirking, said, "Don't you think you had better say goodbye to mom?"

"I walked down the hallway to the kitchen where my mother was washing the dishes. "Mom, I'm leaving home," I announced. "I've packed underwear, socks, a shirt and pants in the bag, and I'm going. I can't stand it here anymore, do you understand? And I'm leaving."

"But where are you going Jeffrey?" my mother asked.

"I don't know yet, but anywhere has got to be better than here. Goodbye!" Without waiting for further comments from my mother, I turned around and walked quickly down the hallway to the living room where my father was still sitting, smirking and smoking his Pall Malls. Mentally, I imagined him winking at my mother over my escapade of running away much as he had winked at me when he "threatened" to beat me. Then he had failed to take my mother seriously. As I walked out the door, I knew that my father didn't take me seriously either.

Again, my father had failed to correct me. It was no skin off his back. If I were so stupid as to run away, then all well and good. Did a man as great as Ellis believed himself to be need a son around who was stupid enough to run away from him? And as for my complaint about the book? What did it matter what I thought? What if I railed and complained? Was leaving home an overreaction, far beyond any mere griping? To Ellis, my pain, and my angry reaction to it, my destructive reaction to it, was laughable and insignificant. To my father, this event was another proof of my weakness and dependence, and of his strength.

Had he not walked past his father at age 17 and left home for good? Had he not proved his masculinity and independence this way? Did I actually believe that at the age of 12 I could accomplish what he was only able to do at 17? His sense of reality told him it was impossible. He had taught me the lesson of independence, of leaving home, but he had taught it to me too early, and had not described the elements of timing, or that you could get a job at 17 when he was a boy, but not at twelve. Like gin rummy, he had taught me the lesson of independence as I studied his life, yet he had not taught me how to be a winner, nor how to step past him, nor when to step past him, as he had stepped past his father.

In my early adolescence I was allowed to grow as an immoral monster. I began going to parties, and found a blossoming interest in girls. I discussed this with my father.

"Dad, you know who's really cute?.... Annette Cohen. I really like her."

"What does she look like Jeffrey?" he asked. "Well, she's little and she has black hair and kind of dark skin."

"Is that the little girl I saw you talking with over at the dance last week? I didn't think she was so cute. She didn't have much on top."

"Well, Gee Dad, what do you want? She's only in sixth grade! Anyhow, I think she's cute...and well, we played spin the bottle at Hoyt's party, and I got to kiss her about 15 times. I tried to see how long I could hold my breath."

My father was smiling broadly. He asked me a few more questions, then teased me because kissing had been the limit of my activities.

"Gee, Dad," I said, flushing red with embarrassment, "we're only 12 years old; we can't do anything like that."

My father burst out laughing. Just then my mother came into the room and he told her what had been said, and she started to laugh too.

I had a big smile on my face too, figuring it must be funny. But I said, "I don't see what's so funny."

"Ellis, I think you had better teach him the facts of life pretty soon," my mother said. "I agree Belle" my father replied. "Next Sunday afternoon, after Omnibus, we'll sit down and I'll explain everything."

My mother walked to the kitchen still chuckling. My father turned to me with a big grin, "Why don't you bring this Annette around here. I'd like to meet her. Maybe I can get her ....more interested."

I flushed red again, but my father kept grinning his know-it-all, lecherous grin.

The wise men who wrote "Proverbs" warned the young men to stay far from the abandoned life of fornication. My father had not read Proverbs. He was not immersed in wisdom, but was burning in the folly of the senses. Growing up meant one thing, and the enactment of our so-called biological urges was for him the end-all and be-all.

My parents ignorantly believed that all I needed was the facts of life to be prepared for what followed in my relations with the opposite sex. Without a commitment to love, to the word of God, and to our Lord and Savior, what else could they think? For them, the sooner I had carnal experience the better. To them, sex was fact, God was imagination and fiction.

How many families in society today are like mine? To say that such a family is neglecting its moral responsibility is to understate the problem. My family was, and many families are today, actively promoting immorality. My family was a training unit, a cell if you will, for the development and training of wrongdoing. Could it be that much of the public handwringing about the youth of society gone wrong is but a cover and a disavowal of parents of not only their failure to bring the kids up right, but of their

actual complicity in the wrong? What should my
parents or any parents do when their son tells them
he is going to parties where the children are playing
kissing games? My parents should have forbidden
me to go to such parties. They should have spent
hours and hours talking to me about the horrors
of indulging the feelings I felt outside of marriage.
Prayer and God's holy word would have been offered
as the essential correctives to a personality gone
astray. Correction, reproof, and prayer were and are
the orders of the day.

Suddenly, at the age of twelve, the pattern of
my relations with my parents changed dramatically.
My father's son by a previous marriage, my half-
brother, in a trick of fate (properly called "God's
providential will" or "His secret counsel") was
assigned by the Post Office to deliver mail in the
neighborhood on his summer mail carrier job. He
had been raised by his mother and stepfather and
grandmother, and Dad had been depicted to him
as a devil. Delivering mail as a man, Myron had a
chance to become acquainted with Dad and to form
his own views. He began regular visits to our home.
Much of the psychic energy in the household shifted
to our relationship with this new, fourth person.
Instead of ranting and raving about my disobedience,
my mother complained, sulked and screamed about
the time my father spent with Myron. Instead of
marathon conversations where my father would
tell me about his union activities, about his sexual
exploits, and about being "a man among men," he

now devoted his time to sharing these boasts with my older half-brother.

"Why do you spend so much time with Myron?!" my mother screamed at my father.

"Oh, here we go again….' My father sneered, taking a drag on his Pall Mall as he sat on his usual spot at the end of the red mohair sofa.

"You never have time to talk to me, you never have time to go to a baseball game with Jeff, you never   have time to go on a vacation, but you have all the time in the world to spend with your... son… Myron! What kind of man are you? What kind of father are you?!"

My father took a puff on his cigarette as he grinned in smirking contempt at my mother during her tirade.

"Are you going or are you not going to go tonight?!" my mother demanded. "Please don't go. I'm asking you… don't go. Don't go!!"

"Of course, I'm going to see Myron tonight, didn't I tell you I was? Don't give me all this stupid — —!! There's no reason why I shouldn't go, and I am going."

My mother was screaming her demands that my father stay home in a rising wailing and sobbing. "DON'T GO ELLIS. DON'T GO. YOU DON'T LOVE ME. WHAT KIND OF MAN ARE YOU? HOW CAN YOU DO THIS TO ME? HOW CAN YOU DO THIS TO ME?!!!"

My father continued to sit there looking at her as she wailed, sobbed and screamed, with a big smirk

on his face. My mother, wailing and sobbing, crying
out for my father not to go to visit Myron, sank to the
floor, and lay there convulsed with sobs and moans
and somehow shouting through the tears and gasps,
"DON'T GO. . . . PLEASE DON'T GO. . . HOW CAN
YOU DO THIS TO ME?. . . ."

My mother knew nothing of the path of grace,
prayer, and God. To her, life was a series of power
struggles where one will and must do anything to get
one's way, to control, and to punish those who deny
one the will and wish of one's heart. She believed
that insistence and aggression were the only paths
to get one's way. The axiom, "Love thy neighbor as
thyself," was not known by her. She had no innate
sense of self-respect. She did not believe in God. She
did not believe that she would be helped by prayer.
She believed that her way was the best way. She did
not believe in a universe ruled by a loving God who
would guide a difficult situation to a just solution,
or that a seemingly unjust resolution could be
redemptive or have ultimately good consequences.

I grew into adolescence a pitiful facsimile of
my parents. Like them, I lacked good emotions.
Like my mother, I had a penchant for hysteria and
insistence. Like my father, I was filled with contempt
and hostility, covered over with superficial smiles
and superficial friendliness and amiability. As with
both of them, I did not believe in God, grace, or
prayer. The thought of Jesus Christ was foreign and
noxious to me. Love? Respect? Perhaps they had a
place somewhere in my mind, but mainly they were

sissified and far from the reality I conceived of as "the world."

As the battle between my parents intensified over my father's relationship with his other son, I forged ahead on a confused path of "personal ambition." However, though ambitious, I did not know what I wanted to be nor what to do. I was governed by an amorphous idea of success. Strongly competitive desires and indecision became the hallmarks of my personality. I believed there were no alternatives to my anxieties nor to my materialistic goals. The Prince of Peace and His path were decades away.

Chapter Four:

Am I Inferior or Superior?

"**G**et away from me you Christ Killer!!" Fritz vehemently shouted these words at me in seventh grade, five weeks into the term. "My father told me that Ludwig is a Jewish name," he said, "and we don't have anything to do with dirty Jews." I was stunned, shocked, confused. In elementary school my playmates had been gentiles and Jews. I knew that the gentiles and I attended different places of worship, but the thought of total, complete rejection for this reason never occurred to me.

The year before I had invited Lucia, a girl in my sixth grade class, to go to a dance at my synagogue. When she asked her mother, she was told that she could not go because it was at a synagogue. That had stunned me, and my parents assured me that her mother was narrow-minded. However, the distancing of Lucia's family from me was neither as threatening nor as horrific as the name calling and violent tone of rejection affirmed by Fritz.

How could it be? Was there really something so poisonous about me? Were all Jews Christ Killers as he said? Why did he hate me so for being a Jew? At the same time, I had practically idolized Fritz. He had come from Germany and was older than the other boys. He was at least five inches taller than the rest of us, and had a level of confidence and "style" that I had never before encountered in one of my classmates.

He had regaled us with stories of his father's heroics as a captain in the German army "during the war." I did not connect this with the Nazi army nor with World War II. To me, he was a storyteller about distant lands and of military feats and of manly courage.

I was a student who was well liked. I had been taunted as a momma's boy, yet, except for sports where I was always the last one picked (I was a year younger than the other students), I was generally cheerful and friendly. I played board games with the other students. And, at parties in sixth grade, I had played the usual kissing games like spin the bottle. I was considered smart. I was also overweight and was suited up in a "husky" size for my bar mitzvah.

On my report card, my sixth grade teacher had written that I worked well individually and in groups. Thus, I did not sense myself as having an adjustment problem.

I did not realize then that as a Jew one automatically has an adjustment problem in life. Some will handle it better than others, but all must deal with it. It is a unique, life changing category. The Jew is uniquely challenged in the world and in American society.

When I encountered Fritz in this mode, for the first time I knew real FEAR. For the first time I knew what it was to be hated by someone. For the first time I learned what it was to be persecuted.

Fritz began to taunt me everyday. "Dirty Jew." "Christ Killer." "Kike." These epithets and others became my daily diet. Threats were heaped upon my head. Sometimes he would push me or punch me in the arm. Sometimes, if he were seated next to me, he would punch me in the leg during class. I was afraid of him. I was afraid of a more serious injury. I was enraged at the public humiliation. He insulted me in front of others, Jews and non-Jews, and I did nothing. I JUST TOOK IT!!

At night I would toss and turn restlessly. I would plot how to kill Fritz. I would think about the possibility of my going to the electric chair. I wanted to ask someone if they thought someone my age would go to the electric chair, or how I would be punished if I killed Fritz. But there was no one to ask. Even as I was afraid of Fritz, I was also afraid to admit that I was afraid.

It seemed to me that my father was such a tough guy that he would be ashamed of me if I admitted that I was afraid. He might tell me to go fight Fritz. Had not my father boasted many times that he was sweeping up outside a grocery store on the day of his brother's wedding when two Italians had called him a "dirty kike," and that he had gotten into a fight with them and had a black eye so he had to wear sunglasses to his brother's wedding? What would he think of a son who would not fight? Fritz was five inches taller than I, and I felt I didn't have a chance;

but I believed that if my father were in my shoes he would not let the height difference intimidate him.

And, if I told my mother, I was afraid she would go to the school and make a fuss. I would be branded even more of a momma's boy for having my mother fight my battles for me.

What was I to do?

One day in mechanical drawing class, Fritz was particularly ferocious in his denunciation of me and of the Jews. Another Jew in the class who wore a large ring told Fritz that he would mash his face if he did not stop bothering him. Fritz immediately stopped. I was so jealous. Why did I not have the guts to make a statement like that and mean it? Yes. I was convinced I was a momma's boy. I lacked guts. I was a weakling…not only physically but, more importantly, I was a weakling morally.

In the same class, Bobby Case, a recent transplant from Texas, was working near my table. Bobby was a rugged lad and a gentile. Fritz was threatening me so much I would hardly do my work. Finally, Bobby spoke up, "Y' all leave him alone, d'y' hear? If you don't ah'm gonna bust ya from here to Texas. Just shuttt yaw mouth Fritz!" Again, Fritz completely backed down, and left me alone for the rest of the period. Bobby had come to my rescue. He was my protector. I felt so relieved, and to this day I am grateful to Bobby.

But the persecutions continued. My grades remained high, but my fear and rage were growing. I was beside myself with hopelessness and helplessness.

One day Fritz was taunting me, and, as he frequently did, he went to punch me in the nose. Usually his fist stopped just short of my nose, and he would laugh in my face. On this occasion, he did not stop his hand in time, and he punched the nose which bled profusely. At least I did not cry. I was proud that I did not cry, but I hurried home with blood all over my T-shirt.

I would no longer be able to hide this persecution from my mother. What would she say? What would she do?

My mother comforted me. She changed my T-shirt. She rubbed my back. Yet, strangely to me, she wasn't hysterical. If I should be playing ball and come into the house sweating a lot, she would be upset almost to the point of hysteria. "You're sweating, you're sweating!!!" And she would berate me for playing so long and hard. She would constantly be picking invisible threads off my clothes and picking invisible specks of dirt out of my ears. She was always after me to do this or that.

Yet, on this occasion, she was surprisingly calm. I even remember her smiling at me as she rubbed my back. When I told her that I did not want her to go to the school, she readily agreed. It was a strange encounter. Only three years before she had gone to school and berated a teacher who had had the nerve to give her perfect boy a "C" for posture.

She comforted me, but offered no suggestions that I recall. She said that she wouldn't tell my father. To this day I do not know why she was so agreeable to my requests.

The problem of Fritz remained. Would I bleed again? Would I actually talk myself into ambushing him and hitting him with a brick?

Sometime during this process, late at night when I could not sleep, I began to pray. I had never been taught to pray. Even though I went to Hebrew school and youth services, prayer was a corporate matter in the Conservative congregation I attended. We were not taught, nor did anyone practice as far as I knew, individual prayer. My father never attended the corporate worship, nor did my mother. I only went so I would keep contact with my friends. I did not want to be alone Saturdays or after school. Besides, it was simply understood that I would be bar mitzvahed at age thirteen.

I began to pray to God to help me and to save me from Fritz. I just prayed, "God, help me; please God stop Fritz from bothering me." My mind would swing from this prayer to fantasies of killing Fritz. Night after night for months, I would exhaust my mind in this way until I finally fell asleep.

Were there no signs of a personality change during this time? Were there no signs that I was suffering so much? Did my parents not see that something was wrong? Did my mother tell my father? And did he decide not to say anything to me? Would it be possible for a little boy to so completely hide such a heart-wrenching experience from his parents for such a long period of time (all of seventh grade)? It seems to me today that it would not be possible, and that my parents decided not to intervene, and to allow events to unfold. It seemed to me that my father's answer would be one answer – I would have to fight him, and if I did not take this one and only practical step then I would have to face the consequences until I saw that there was no other way and faced up to the situation.

Finally, as the school year drew to a close, three weeks before the end of the term, Fritz disappeared. Fritz disappeared!! He had moved across the river to live in New Jersey. I would go into eighth grade free of Fritz! To my mind this was an answered prayer. I had told no one that I prayed, so this answer was like the entire problem itself, experienced alone, a secret difficulty solved by God and known only to God and me.

Yet God was himself a secret, and His nature and existence was not discussed even in Sunday school or Hebrew school. Rather God was portrayed as one voice or character in the saga of the Jewish people In our lessons, the Jewish people were center stage, not God, and if we prayed together it was because we are Jews and that is what we do and have always done, and not because of God. We just want to keep on being Jews, so we just keep on praying and keep on studying. Being a Jew was one piece with these activities, and God was simply working in some remote way to support our aims.

However, the emotional hurts of that sorry year did not disappear along with Fritz. The shame I experienced having been insulted so regularly, and the sense of helplessness I felt in my dealings with him left me feeling drained, discouraged, and mistrustful of others and myself. I had liked Fritz, but he had suddenly turned on me and become my enemy. After he left, I was relieved, but I felt dirty, inadequate, unmanned, and a note of anxiety and fear of the future seemed to enter my personality.

I vowed never to let such an event happen again. I vowed that should another Fritz come into my life, I would indeed fight him. I would fight him and fight to the death if need be rather than accept such humiliation. But I would not die. No, I resolved that next time – NEXT TIME (O God forbid!!) – I would destroy Fritz. I would take him apart limb from limb. I would wipe up the floor with him. I would find a way. I would be more determined. I would be more fierce. I would take the action I knew my father would have taken, only I would be strategic. I would plan everything so carefully I couldn't lose. In short, even though Fritz left, I continued to dream about torturing and killing Fritz. The wound inside me burned and burned. The rage I felt towards Fritz was burning inside me day after day, month after month, year after year. It was a secret anger, a secret burning, a secret hate, a secret reality. Maybe God knew, and maybe he did not? Maybe he had answered my prayers (it seemed He had); but whether he had or not, the one thing I knew was that hate.

The one thing I knew was that such an event must never happen again. The one thing I knew was that I would be watchful FOREVER that such an event would never happen again. NO. NO. NO.

Dear reader, I was determined that it would NEVER HAPPEN AGAIN.

The school year with Fritz was a life-changing experience. To be on the receiving end of hate and violence challenges the whole personality, wounds the whole personality. Of course there were options open to me. I might have gone to the principal or to my teachers. I might have told my father and asked him to go to the school to talk to the teachers. Perhaps I was wrong in assessing his reaction or expectations. Or I might have fought Fritz even taking a worse beating but "saving face."

Whatever might have been the outcome, I internalized the pain. I lost my childhood innocence and trust. I changed my philosophy of life. I determined that I would get even. Getting even became a theme in my personality. Outwardly I was still smiling, but inwardly despondency, gloom, and self-disgust had found a place.

My relationship with other friends began to change. When we would engage in youthful roughhousing, I became more aggressive. When Joe began to harass me in woodshop, I threw the eraser back, and had to stay after school. Another day he began to punch me against the wall. Then I walloped him back a few good ones, and he ran away. I told myself that I cannot continue being a "scared kid." I must fight back! I must assert myself!

My experience with Fritz taught me that if I was insulted and persecuted and harmed I am inferior. My conclusion was that if one persecuted and insulted another, he or she must be superior. Yet, at the same time, I somehow had a moral sense which told me that being a bully is wrong. The way to really be superior was to fight back, to stop the aggression of others, to defeat any and all bullying, but at the same time not to become a bully.

Years later, at the age of eighteen, I was working a summer postal job as a mail clerk. I had passed the mail clerk examination, and was appointed to work at the U.S. Post Office. During that year, first class mail was delivered by railroad, and during the summer, there was a railroad strike. Mail was transferred to trucks, and one night all the clerks were herded into trucks and taken from the Post Office to the warehouse to unload the mail trucks. After doing this for a couple of hours, I went to my supervisor and said that I had passed the mail clerk examination, and was not a mail handler, and that I did not want to unload the trucks.

Although we had not been told this was an optional assignment when we were taken, the supervisor, without hesitating, put me on a truck back to the Post Office where I could be a clerk. The work had not been put before us as a volunteer assignment. Rather we were sent to meet the demands of the situation. The lesson I had learned from my dealings with Fritz came to the fore in that situation. I would not be pushed around or used. I was sensitive and supersensitive on this point. I would not try to tell the other men to walk off their jobs, but I would not participate if I felt that I was being unfairly used. No one, not even my own government would be pushing me around.

Any event that would intervene to disturb my peace and harmony with my surroundings was perceived as a threat to my well-being. Every event was seen through the filtered glass of the Fritz experience. The whole world eventually began to appear more and more to me as a big bully that was invading my dignity, my right to be me, my right to co-exist with others. Needless to say, my favorite book in college was *1984* by George Orwell. That book traces the Orwellian nightmare fantasy of totalitarian rule where "big Brother' is constantly watching over one's every move and attempting to destroy any and every vestige of individuality and dignity that a person may have, using one's every move as an excuse for possible reprisal and even execution.

And year after year I dreamed of Fritz. I am going to look for him. I am going to find him. I'm going to kill him. No one will believe I did it or look for me. It will appear as a motiveless crime. Why? Because who would think to go back to seventh grade to explain why someone is murdered? Who would even believe that a child that age could harbor so much anger that it would last into adult life and through many intervening experiences? Yet, dear friends, that is exactly what happened. I continued to nurture my desire for revenge against Fritz even as many years passed. Does this sound bizarre to you? Well, then so be it, because friends it is true. Every word I am writing is true.

No matter what happened, I could not find satisfaction because my parents and teachers were pleased with my progress, I continued to feel deep down inferior and inadequate and helpless and hopeless because of what had happened in that year of association with Fritz.

No matter what happened, I could not find satisfaction because my desire for revenge against Fritz was continually unsatisfied. I could not feel like a man because I felt that I had been unmanned in that conflict; I could not think of anything except this terrible event. I often would tell my friends about it, but the depth and extent of this event's influence over my life was never made known to others, and indeed, even I underestimated the impact of those events in my life.

I will never forget. I must never forget. It must never happen again. I will get even. I must get even.

And then when I was twenty-one, I visited Germany. I visited Hamburg, and I visited Munich. While a student in England, I even was friends with another German student, Ernst, and we had travelled together to Morocco. What kind of revenge is this, I asked myself. I wondered how I could be visiting Germany after having known Fritz. How could I be friends with Ernst? Was I a sucker? A fool? It seemed my life was unbelievably complex.

Germans murdered the Jews. Fritz persecuted me. How could I visit Germany? How could I be friends with a German? Yet, I knew too that I was civilized, educated. The way of civilization and

education is tolerance, not the way of hate. The
way of education is not to over-generalize. One bad
experience with Fritz doth not a people make. This
is a new era. It is post-war Europe, post-war Germany,
and I am a surviving post-War Jew. I cannot continue
carrying my Fritz-phobia so strongly, and so far,
into all relationships. Yet…there was a conflict. The
Fritz phobia did not go away, and when I heard the
German graduate students, who were certainly anti-
Nazi, say, at the same time, that Hitler had built some
good highways, a deep fire was ignited in my Heart.
Are we fellow graduate students? Are we enlightened,
educated young men together. No. DEATH TO
GERMANY!! DEATH TO…YOU!!

Fritz's epithet "Christ Killer" was always ringing in
my ears The Jews didn't kill Christ, and even if they
had, that was two thousand years ago! Why should
that come up in mechanical drawing class, or any
other time? I would not kill anybody, let alone Christ.
What a disgusting and wrongheaded thing to say!!

Yes, my behavior was educated and tolerant. I
had channeled my aggressions into constructive
activities. The dean of the graduate school I attended
declared in a reference that I was "progressive." I
was vigorous, outspoken, aggressive, bright, and
a gentleman. Fritz should have been forgotten
years ago. His name should just have been part of a
repulsive and unfortunate childhood episode. But
friends, "should" is just another word in the English
language. The reality is far different. The poisonous
and self-destroying feelings that were engendered

during that seventh grade did not disappear. Rather, they were hidden away deep within my heart. They were festering. They were terrible.

I was far from Christ. I was a Jewish atheist. I was educated. I believed in textbooks and the university as the receptacle of all truth. Ph.D.'s were my priests and my Gods. I was advancing in education. I was on my way to becoming one of those "Gods." [sic]

Yet, one day I was writing an essay in my room. It was based on the experience of a beatnik poet who had written about his experience of visiting India. In one of his poems, he wrote about lying on a wooden bed in a hut in India and compared himself to Christ on the Cross. As I wrote the name Jesus Christ in my essay, the first time in my life I had written that name, I fainted and fell off my chair. "Jesus Christ . . . Jesus Christ. . . . " His name reverberated through my mind. Other words, strange words in foreign languages came to my lips, came into my mind, kept reappearing in my dreams. I wrote some of those words on sheets of paper and hung them around the room. *Ahimsa. Schumayacha. Maranatha.* None of these words meant anything to me. I never heard them or any words like them.

Suddenly it seemed to me that I believed in Christ. My heart was open to Christ. But my conscious mind rebelled. Christ? I don't know anything about Christ. What about all that I have learned? What about poetry? Mysticism? Philosophy? Where did all these fit in? and besides, and besides – Fritz had called me a Christ killer? Where does all this fit? The pieces of the puzzle were a jumble in my mind. I did not know what to believe. I did not know how to phrase my questions.

Then a period, a long period, followed when I believed that Christ existed (my father had insisted that He was a fictional character like Superman), and that he had great teachings about forgiveness. I kept trying to merge Christ with other writings with which I was familiar and with concepts that were part of my intellectual baggage.

Yet, through it all, there was a deep wish. I deeply wished that I could meet Christ and address this one great question to him: am I a Christ killer? Was Fritz right in saying that to me? And I began to think about how great it would be if I could meet Jesus Christ and if he would agree to go with me to Fritz and to testify to Fritz that indeed I was not a Christ killer, and that Fritz had been dead wrong. It was like looking for the one perfect witness in a law case who can prove your client is innocent. Jesus Christ himself would prove to Fritz in a way I never could that he was wrong, and that "proof" would cause Fritz to feel sorry for what he had done to me.

Indeed, what I wanted more than anything at that time was not mainly revenge on Fritz but for him to apologize to me, to admit that he had wronged me, and to express the desire to make it up to me for the hurt and years of pain that had followed these childhood experiences. If I still thought of torturing him, it was not the thought of torture for torture's sake or to get even, but to torture him to the point where he would admit being wrong. Perhaps I would combine this torture with Jesus being present telling him that he was wrong, and that I was not a Christ Killer and that he should have been ashamed of himself instead of making me ashamed of myself for accepting so many humiliations.

Yes. I wanted to transfer my sense of shame and humiliation and self-hatred to Fritz. Jesus Christ and/or torture would be the mechanism for affecting that transfer.

Surely you, dear reader, know better than I did at that time that the perverse wishes of a sick soul cannot be realized. The only effect is to twist the soul into deeper realms of unhappiness. No wonder I could not find satisfaction in life. I was dreaming, deep within, of finding a satisfaction to a situation that had long since passed, and in ways that were not only "unrealistic" but wrong.

You cannot force someone to say they are sorry (and mean it). If you do, the apology is insincere. And even if the apology is sincere, their apology cannot force you to forgive them. The challenge is: what is my attitude towards Fritz, not what is his attitude towards me.

Friends, I had to keep going through the murky zone of unbelief and half-truths. The theme of Fritz-hatred was only one of many bottled up, secret themes in my personality that could not be resolved. Altogether they comprised a personality gordian knot that could neither be untangled nor unraveled by therapists, study, writing, painting, psychodrama, travel, or wine. This pit was caused by sin, but my anti-religious, atheistic mindset denied the existence of "sin." To me, it was a mythical category created by outdated clerics. So many roads were travelled by me in futile attempts to unravel the pain, and to exorcise the troubling troubles and hurtful hurts of my past that were ongoing in my present. And even my attempts to cast Jesus Christ as the arbiter in the inner war seemed to fail.

Why did all my attempts to "reach out to God" fail? The answer simply put is that I wanted to control the Holy Spirit of the Living God. I wanted to tell Jesus what he was supposed to tell me and what he was supposed to tell Fritz and do to Fritz and all other supposed malefactors in my life. I did not accord Jesus the love and respect of allowing Him to speak for Himself. I did not allow the Holy Word of God, the Holy Bible, to speak to my heart. I did not allow the forgiveness of God, that Holy Spirit of comfort and peace to invade my inner being. Even when I began to believe in Christ, I was running from Him. The Hound of Heaven was pursuing, but I was running away.

"Fritz: it is not over; it is not over," I often told myself. I told myself that I was coming to get him, and people like him also, and that I would be coming with Jesus Christ. Jesus Christ was like the father or big brother who was going to beat up on Fritz with me. We were going to get Fritz, and then he would be sorry he did what he did and said what he said to me. The next time we met, it would be his blood that would be spilled.

But then, dear friends, a day came when I understood that Jesus Christ is not in the business of abetting my sick schemes. On that day I realized that Jesus told Peter to put up his sword. On that day I realized that Jesus shed his own precious blood that I might experience the complete forgiveness for my sins. On that day I realized that I am the problem, not Fritz. On that blessed day I realized that my years of hurt and hate based on an injustice were hurting me, destroying me, and that was Satan's plot. No one was being hurt but me. I was the one in need of healing. I was the one in pain. I was the one who was so concerned about looking bad or appearing to be inferior or being inferior that I could not see the great truth that the least in the Kingdom of Heaven is greater than the greatest of those on earth. Jesus Christ came for my sins and not to avenge me. He came for Fritz too. Fritz also has the opportunity to repent for his sins and to be forgiven by Jesus Christ and to know eternal life.

This is the great abiding truth: Jesus Christ is our Personal Savior. He comes to save you and he comes to save me. We come before Him as individuals in need of forgiveness, in need of healing, in need of hope, and in need of everlasting life which gives that hope.

The Bible tells us that to as many as received Him he gave them the power to call on His Name and to become children of God (John 1:12).

One blessed day, I received Jesus Christ as my personal Savior, and as Lord of my life. And on that day, not surprisingly, I was saved. I was saved from my hate and hurt regarding Fritz, and I was saved for eternal life with Jesus Christ, from my damnable fear of being inferior (pride).

Was I humiliated and publicly demeaned by Fritz? The answer of course is yes. Do I have to kill him in order to have hope? To make up for the events I despised? The answer is an absolute NO. There is no hope for me in my hate. Indeed, if hate were the hope then where would the cycle of hate and killing end? And if it were not to end, then where is the hope? Dear friends, the light of the True and Living God has entered my heart. Jesus Christ is the Way, the Truth, and the Life. Love Him, and accept His testimony that He is the Messiah, the Son of God and worthy to be worshipped. Accept Him and love Him and receive Him today, and be saved.

Chapter Five:

Grace and Neurosis

I was a child who did not know nor had been taught to "Honor Thy Father and Thy Mother." This simple "shall" of the Ten Commandments is such a gold mine of meaning, full of hope, and pointing the way to proper child-parent relations. Is it not our tendency to use psychology today? A certain author, Haim Ginott, wrote a bestselling book where he describes various verbal strategies whereby the parent can give the "best" response to this or that behavior of his/her child. The idea of the book is that the parent may be able to communicate the love or respect the parent feels in a way that the child will understand. The premise of the book is that certain modes of address to children are more readily accepted by the child than others. Yet, something more is at stake in the upbringing of the child than is fathomed by the author of the psychology book. The "something more" is the receiving of a blessing from God, or favor from God. The entire commandment of God reads, "Honor thy father and mother that thy days may be long upon the land." How does one receive a long life? One only receives a long life in and through the blessing of God. The reference to long life here then does not involve us in special diets or exercise programs, nor does the blessing of life come from forms of meditation. Rather, the blessing of a long life comes from honoring one's father and mother.

This commandment was addressed to the children of Israel. It is addressed to all ages, though the assumption is that the individuals to whom it is addressed have reached the age of understanding. Many of those reading or hearing this commandment might themselves be parents. So, the first thing any parent must ask himself or herself is what is her relationship with and attitude towards his or her parent. Is the attitude and relationship based on love? Or is it based on convenience? Is there a strong undercurrent of hostility? Or is there unforgiveness for past wrongs? Are the parents shunted aside in an old age home and visited once a year at Passover, Rosh Hashanah, or Christmas? Is there continuous communication with the parent? Are visits exchanged? Is the relationship a friendly one? Or are there many arguments? The younger children will observe and learn attitudes towards their parents from what they observe in the relationship their parents have with their grandparents. Amen. Jesus told his followers, "A new commandment do I give you to love one another as I HAVE LOVED YOU." What a great love is this? This saying shows the power of example among many things. We do not learn to love from an abstraction or definition of love, nor from a theory of love no matter how exquisitely crafted. We learn to love from the example of love that has been given to our lives.

Thus, love may be handed down from generation to generation. At the same time, the love of God himself comes into our lives, into the lives of each individual in every generation, in and through the grace of God, through the working of the Holy Spirit. Thus, through grace, we may honor our parents. Even if we have not experienced growing up in a loving home, God Almighty will teach us the paths of love and the patience and humility needed to follow those paths.

The Lord knocks. His grace is sufficient, yet we bear responsibility for accepting or rejecting this grace. "Knock and it shall be opened unto you." God Almighty is knocking; yet we are to experience ourselves as the 'knockers' and thus take responsibility for our "own" actions which express the grace that we seek and accept. Thank you Lord.

The relationship between parent and child cannot be separated from grace, love of God, and prayer. These are the keys to a successful parent-child relationship. Speech is secondary. Perfecting the verbal communication is an empty shell or form of Godliness, but without the power. The power to honor, the gift of honoring, one's parents comes from God. We must seek it from God. We must bring up a child in the way he should go.

Thus, my argumentativeness and hostility were verbal manifestations of a deeper spiritual sickness. I was sin sick. I lacked grace, the love of God, and prayer. Without these my life was formless and filthy. The Hebrew word for honor also might be translated "glorify." (*kavod*).. Without giving God Almighty the glory in our home, the foul spirit of the antichrist possessed me. I was a little version of the lawless one. I did not know the spirit of the higher commandment of Love, and thus broke the simple commandment to speak to my mother with love.

You see *kinder* (children), many Jewish boychiks growing up face a certain problem. It might be a problem or it might be a crazy mess ("*mishegoss*"). Mishegoss is an insanity, a madness. ... but it does not appear in any psychiatric textbook. It is a type of madness that defies psychiatry. And rightly so because we know that it is He and He alone that heals *mishegoss*, and not the M.D.'s with their secret sessions.

You see *kinder*, many Jewish boychiks grow up with a mama problem. I mean: a Jewish mama, so who could love a son more? I mean: so he's my son, maybe I'm not perfect, but who is? . . . Nobody knows how a mother feels . . . .

Not every Jewish mother is THE Jewish mother type. And not every son is driven *messhuge* ("crazy") by his relationship with his Jewish mother. Much has been written on the subject: words like "oedipal," "separation anxiety," "possessiveness," "power struggle," "domineering," "insecurity," and "obsession." Comedians have joked about it. Writers like Philip Roth have tried to portray this subject in a light vein.

Not yet, no, not yet *kinder*, has the right balance been struck between humor and seriousness for this subject. This *mishegoss* is still waiting to be understood. "Mama, leave me alone already . . . yes, I know you mean well, but . . . . I mean, I'm a grown man, you just . . . . well, don't act this way towards a grown man . . . . ."

Only Yeshua's great love showed me how to break the gordian knot of this intrapsychic problem. To paraphrase William Shakespeare, "whether tis nobler in mind to suffer the slings and arrows of outrageous *mishegoss*, or to die...." Yes, my dear *machetunnim* ("family members"), oy vey and oy vey, I was myself driven into deep pools of inner turmoil, and into slow day-by-day mental torment over the relationship that I had or did not have with my Yiddisha momma.

To her, I was alternately king and *schlemiel* ("jerk"). Nothing I could do was right. It seemed she was always checking my ears, my buttons, my zipper, my collar, my coat, my hat, my shoes. I was under daily inspection, and I was daily falling short. Yet, at the same time I was her little adored prince. On Saturdays, she would fix me American cheese, mayonnaise and onion sandwiches (with a side of Heinz baked beans), which she would serve me on a little metal tray with a floral design while I watched five to eight hours of TV. Sometimes, even during the week, she would bring me dinner in the living room so I could watch TV and eat, or

I would do my homework and watch TV. Especially in matters of TV, I was indulged. No TV was too much TV, and as long as I was getting good marks in school, so why not?. . . .

Yet, how many fights did we have over her following me to the bathroom and sitting on the side of the bathtub reading a story to me, or just sitting, while I did my #2 duty. One side of me felt like King Tut sitting on his throne, a holy and special set-aside person whose every stool was a matter of great interest. Yet, this was a deep down reaction. Consciously, I felt humiliated. I would beg her to stay out. I could go myself. Yet, in she would come until I was twelve years old. I would sit there doing my business. She would often read a story to me to help me go, or run the water in the sink if I were constipated, or give me a suppository (are you surprised I was constipated?), and then, when I was finished, would inspect the debris visually for color or signs of blood from straining. She would take a metal clothes hanger and fluff the matter until she was satisfied that it was all as it should be.

If my friends ever found out! O my, o my! I would never be able to go out of the house. I would be a laughing stock to the whole world. It was bad enough that they said I was a momma's boy. It was bad enough that they saw her always looking over my shoulder, always on my case, but THIS!! If they ever found out, if they ever found out, if they ever found out . . . IT (my life, my self-respect, my dignity, my pride) would all be gone. Yes, now, sixty years later, it can be revealed, through the grace and mercy of God's love, that for twelve years, I rarely did my duty alone. I had my own home attendant, with large brown eyes, and a concerned, worried expression on her face, who watched over my every contraction, my every movement.

Chapter Six:

Hebrew School Wisdom

It was never my parents' intention to send me to Hebrew school. My father associated all things Jewish with the harsh rule he had had under his father. His father demanded uncompromising obedience and attention in the synagogue and outside. His father was a religious Jew who loved hanging around the synagogue exchanging stories of the "old world" with his fellow Russian Jews.

My mother went along with my father in these matters. She had not grown up in a strictly Jewish home, and my guess is that she did not try to keep a more Jewish home more out of laziness than out of a desire to comply with the anti-religious attitudes of my father. Two sets of dishes, lighting candles, learning prayers, going to synagogue, relating to other people, involved too much of her personality and too much work.   She was a person who did not like to go out of the house, who did not like to have visitors, who did not have friends, and who, in short, avoided life. In the house she was mistress of all she surveyed. As queen, she need not brook any opposition or "other ways." Her ways were supreme. There would be no Sabbath Queen, only Belle, the Queen of 5831 Beaumont Street.

Yet, all my friends began attending Hebrew school three times a week when they reached the age of ten, two afternoons a week after school, and then on Sunday mornings. This discipline also required attendance for three hours on Saturday mornings at the junior congregation service at Beth Am synagogue at 58th and Warrington Avenues.

I had no friends to play with after school except those who were in Hebrew school. So I began to attend. Barry, Phil, and Mark were there.

We learned our Hebrew from Mr. Kornblatt. He told my mother that if he had a son, he would want his son to be like me.

When I was 12, I began preparing for my bar mitzvah. I had to go to extra classes to learn my portion from the Torah ("*haftorah*") including the sounds of the chants. Marvin and I were to be bar mitzvahed (a ceremony for 13 year old boys accepting responsibility before God for their ritual and personal behavior as Jews) at the same service. Marvin kept insisting that he was going to do his *haftorah* better than I would do mine. I could not understand why he was competing with me. It seemed clear to me that there was no "better" for the bar mitzvah. Each boy had a certain level to reach. Each had to do his best. We were to be prepared, and we were prepared. There were no grades given for *haftorah* or for chanting.

JL At 12 Years Old Prior to Bar Mitzvah

The day in June came. The relatives from the two families all showed up proudly to watch their boys.

I chanted my portion. Marvin's turn came and he forgot the words and the chants. His presentation began to crumble as he succumbed to stage fright. I wondered if God had caused this to happen to teach Marvin a lesson. I genuinely had no interest in seeing him stumble. And why would he stumble? He was a bright fellow. He had prepared for months the same as I. Yet he stumbled and fumbled his way through. I felt certain that all his boasting had something to do with it. Only years later would I read the words of Jesus, "those who exalt themselves will be humbled and those who humble themselves will be exalted."

During my years in Hebrew school I learned to read the book of Genesis in Hebrew. Then, after my bar mitzvah, I decided to drop out. The students in class were unruly, I was busy coping with the demands of Central High School, and I had begun going to parties on weekends so it was more difficult for me to wake up on time Saturday and Sunday mornings.

The rabbi was irate. "How can you as a mother permit this?!" he shouted at my mother over the telephone. He offered everything to keep me in attendance.

"Our wish," he told her "is that he will finish Hebrew high school, and then go on to Hebrew college [both running classes at the same time I would be going to regular high school and college]. Who knows? He might be a candidate for the rabbinate?"

"Finances," he asserted, "should not be an issue." The rabbi said that all costs would be assumed by the synagogue and the Conservative movement. If there was any issue of money, we need not worry about anything. They could not lose a boy like me.

The rabbi asked that a meeting be arranged with him and me. My father, with visions of his violent childhood environment, imagined the worst. "If the rabbi hits you, I swear I'll go over there and beat him up." He still remembered the teachers and rabbis of the *cheders* ("Hebrew schools") of his childhood feeling free to strike the students. My macho father stood ready to beat up any rabbi he met!

Needless to say, I met with the rabbi, and we had a heart-to-heart talk. He was kindly, and repeatedly tried to persuade me not to drop out of my Hebrew studies. He stressed my Jewish heritage, my abilities, my opportunities to help the Jewish community, my need to be an active participant in Jewish life, and many other matters. Over and over again he came back to the question, will you change your mind? Although I felt my resolve waver somewhat, I stubbornly refused to reconsider. I did not argue with him. I politely and repeatedly stated that I did not believe I would continue.

Yes, I loved to dance the *horah* (a Jewish group circle dance) with the youth group. I loved the services that were led by the youth. I loved learning an arcane language and thereby feeling different and special.

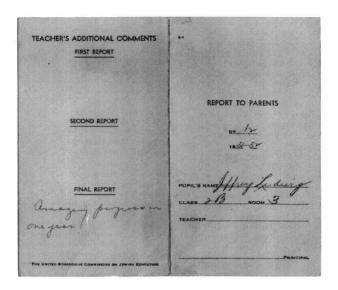

JL Hebrew School Report Card

But ultimately I decided, why bother? I had gone to another high school out of the neighborhood, and my friendships with those in the neighborhood were no longer essential. I was facing new academic challenges at Central High, and decided to let the old friendships die. Attendance at Hebrew school did not seem to win me any points with my parents, especially my father, who looked upon all religion as a somewhat unpleasant dispensation in the universe. My mother cried when the rabbi scolded her, but she was indifferent to all matters Jewish. Her entire mental life seemed to revolve around certain negative obsessions: her stepmother, our family's relationship with my older half-brother fathered by my father in his first marriage, her disagreements with certain members of my father's family, and her relationship with me and my father, largely based on complaining (although on some joyous occasions she would join us for a card game, or play checkers with me or the card game "Fish"). Sometimes she would just talk or watch TV with us and laugh at some comedy. Those times were a joy to me. She would just be "normal." I loved to hear my mother laugh. Sometimes she would rub my back. That's when I really felt she cared.

She had no friendships, no outside interests, no charitable interests, no hobbies, no spiritual or religious interests, no interest in reading, music, or art, no favorite TV shows or radio shows, and, as far as I know to this day, no favorite foods, although I surmise that boiled chicken or chicken salad were at the top of her list.

Now, I love her dearly. Yet, I know at the same time, she was a one-track minded, fear ridden and unhappy individual who did not know how to or care to reach out to others, even my father or me. She had a lonely spirit (I inherited it). She did not feel that she fit in. Probably she didn't. The expectation became father to the deed.

My father mocked her for "going upstairs to make the bed." She would go upstairs to make the bed, but instead she would take a nap and reappear a few hours later. She was overweight. She tired easily. Her worries tired her out. Her worries were many. She had, over the years, forgotten the relaxed mood of the slow dance.

Chapter Seven:

My Father

M y father was 5'7" in height, thickly set, and his expression was dominated by a large, square, firmly set jaw with a cleft in the middle. He had a large nose, a ruddy complexion and merry blue eyes. As a young man, when fellow Jews met him at first they would think he was a *shaygetz* ("male non-Jew") because of the blue eyes, but once he began speaking with them in Yiddish they realized he was one of them.

He worked as a trolley car motorman, conductor, and later, as a bus driver for the Philadelphia municipal transit system. His father had also been a motorman and conductor.

Material needs were provided for in our home on a modest scale, but there were no spiritual values. My parents never attended synagogue services, and as far as Christianity went, my father did not believe Jesus Christ ever existed. To him, the existence of Yeshua was a fiction propounded by ingenious minds for their own purposes. And what about Moses? If there were a Moses, surely the truth about him had been embellished. The Red Sea Parting? Simply unbelievable. If there was a God – as a good agnostic he entertained the remote possibility – he was a kind of "force."

"This run for chairman of Callowhill is going to be a rough one, but I think I can win." My father was telling my mother and me about his plans to run for chairman, the equivalent of shop steward, of the bus depot. The bus drivers worked out of different depots and every two years elected four men to represent them.

My father's two favorite topics of conversation were his activities in the union and his strength and sexual exploits as a young man.

We sat in the kitchen. The wallpaper had red roosters perched in front of clocks. The table top was green and white. A brown Motorola table radio was on the table top. My father smoked his Pall Malls and flicked his ashes into a square glass ashtray. My mother washed the dishes in a stainless steel, single-basin sink.

"O'Hara's hard to beat. He's got this tight Catholic vote. He sees a lot of these guys in church. They know him.

"But," he continued, "O'Hara is dumb. He doesn't know anything – about insurance, pensions, how to fill out an accident report, union rules or benefits. If the men ask him a question, he has to come to me to get the answer."

"Well, dad," I asked, "If that's the case, why does he get any votes at all? Don't the men want to have a chairman who knows things, knows about the things that count?"

"This O'Hara, see, Jeff, he's what they call a 'do-gooder'. He goes to the hospital to visit the men when they're sick, or if somebody in their family is sick. He goes to the wakes. And they all went to Catholic schools and know the priests and things like that. You know, they like him, but at the same time, they know he's stupid. So I have to work on that."

"I can see that Dad," I piped in, "going to hospitals is o.k., but that doesn't pay the bills – I mean you can be somebody's friend, but if you want to be a union officer, you have to know something more than the other guys about the job, about making a living."

"Exactly," my father said, adding, "that's exactly the point. These do-gooders like Leo, they want to help people, but they don't know anything – it's like buttering up people – it's all gooey...I care, we're brothers, and all that stuff – but when it all comes down to it, guys like O'Hara are just as much for number one as everybody else. So you go visit somebody in a hospital. What's it worth? In dollars and cents what's it worth? It's just a gesture, just another way to get a vote...and these suckers, a lot of them go for it."

My father, you see, had contempt for any acts of mercy, love, or kindness. If he had ever known the Hebrew word *chesed* ("lovingkindness") in his youth when he regularly attended *cheder* ("Hebrew school") and *schul* ("synagogue"), then surely he had forgotten it. Everyone, he believed, lived for money and power and to try to satisfy the insatiable demands of his ego and material cravings. Any acts of mercy or kindness were written off by him as "mere hypocrisy." Those who felt they needed such acts or who found comfort in such acts or were loyal to those who performed such acts were considered by him to be "suckers."

My father put himself at the center of his universe. His goal was to convince the men in the bus depot that Leo O'Hara's caring was not caring, but stupidity – that a vote for O'Hara was not a vote for a friend, for a fellow Christian and good neighbor, but a vote for ignorance, and ultimately a vote for the kinds of mistakes which ultimately would cause the men harm. My father wholeheartedly gave himself over to the deceit that a well-filled-out form is more important to the well-being of a man than the concern, interest, and attention of a friend.

Be warned dear reader, lest such a view be controlling your life today. The Lord (yes, God Almighty) has commanded us to "Love your neighbor as yourself." And Our Savior, *Yeshua*, during His last days on this earth told his followers, "A new commandment do I leave you: to love one another as I have loved you." Yes, in the New Covenant (New Testament), we are commanded by Almighty God to go far beyond mere acts of mercy and kindness, but to love one another as God's Son loved us. We are to take on the heart of God, the mind of Christ himself, and to sacrifice all, following the Living Word of God home to heaven.

What were my father's motives for learning about pensions, insurance, worker legislation, etc.? I believe

that his motive was to make himself a hero. He did
not read up on tax laws or pensions with a true desire
to help (for every desire to help is based on the love
of God – "seek ye first the kingdom of God and his
righteousness, and all these shall be added unto you").
Rather, I believe he desired to impress others that he
was smart in order that he might be elected to union
office –the avenue to the gravy train that he coveted.
He gave his knowledge in order to GET. Not only did
he wish to get their votes, but he would often charge
his co-workers for his help in filling out their accident
reports. Greed, lust, pride, and a deep down selfishness
–an utterly narrow desire for personal gain – lay at the
heart of his style of unionism. Where was Jesus Christ?
Where was the Ten Commandments? Where was love?
O, Lord have mercy! Woe to every man who walks his
daily walk with such a jaded, cynical, and sinful attitude
of heart and mind!!!

Dear reader: I ask you right now: are you
drowning in iniquity? Have you been hypnotized
by the color green and ink drawings of George
Washington, Andrew Jackson, or Benjamin Franklin?
Has your heart been hardened against your fellow
man? Stop then. Reconsider. Reflect. Hear the Good
News. It doesn't have to be this way. God loves you,
and he is calling to you today to follow him, follow
the way of *Yeshua Hamaschiach* ("Jesus the Christ").

Sadly, the path of love and Godliness was not Ellis
Ludwig's path. He preferred the stealing, womanizing
and thuggery of the union. He boasted of his wild
youth. He indulged prideful fantasies of being "smart

for a bus driver." He railed against and mocked all believers, making no distinctions. Smirking and laughing, his daily monologues were a running repudiation of holiness and the Truth of God.

He boasted of knowing bookies, of gambling (cards, horses, checkers for money), or buying stolen goods and of associating with assorted thugs.

He believed that his life represented the triumph of tough-minded me-first realism over the hypocritical, God-believing world which is controlled, as he thought, by management, the power brokers of politics and other educated phonies. He did not understand and did not want to understand that this world is controlled from on high. He did not understand and did not want to understand that "we wrestle not against flesh and blood, but against powers, against principalities, against the rulers of darkness, and against wickedness in high places."

"Dad, last night I got a ticket, a moving violation," I told my father forlornly. I had been driving the family car, and on my way home from a party, I had been pulled over by the police who said that I had run a red light.

"What happened Jeff? Where did you get the ticket?" he asked.

"At 55th & Springfield. I went through a light, and the police said that I ran the red. I thought it had turned orange when I was about 1/3 into the intersection."

"Well, don't worry about it," he replied. "We can fix it."

"What do you mean Dad?" I asked. "Aren't these the new 'no fix' tickets that they wrote about in the newspapers a couple of months ago?"

My father smirked and chuckled. "That's just a news story for all the do-gooders. The thing is, see, you have the ticket – it's for $15, right.

"Well, if you pay it, there's no hearing, and it doesn't go on your record."

"Yes."

"O.K. Now if you don't pay it within 60 days, you get a summons, and you have to go to court. If you go this route, it can get tricky. So let's say you go to court, and you lose your case – then you have to pay $65 for the ticket, and it goes on your record – you get points, and it will affect your insurance and could count against you if there are future violations."

"Yes, I see: IT'S RISKY NOT TO PAY THE $15."

"But here's the point: it's only risky if it's risky. Vito at the union can get to anyone. The judges are in our pocket, or some of them are anyhow. We just arrange it through Jacobs to get you in front of the right judge."

"Then what happens Dad?" I asked.

"Then you go in the judge asks you a couple of questions, maybe the cop who ticketed you will be there – don't worry, I'll tell you what to say before you go in – and then the judge says 'not guilty' or 'case dismissed' and you go home."

"But, Dad, you know I'm not sure that I really would get fined if I got a hearing. I mean it's a question of whether or not I really ran that light."

"Don't be stupid. It doesn't matter. Why take chances? Do you think the judge cares whether you ran the light or not. It doesn't matter one way or the other, so the thing to do is just to tell the judge that you need a favor and let the kid off, and he goes along. We do things for him; he does things for us."

"It's as easy as that?" I asked, amazed that a judge could be so easily manipulated.

"It's as easy as that. Vito has a lot of connections in South Philly. He may be a sneaky rat, but I tell you that guy really has connections. He can even get to Congressmen. Believe me, there's nothing to it."

"O.K., then," he said with an air of finality. "Where's that ticket? Tear it up and throw it in the garbage."

Two months later I received a summons to appear in court about my unpaid ticket. Three weeks after that, I appeared before the judge. The policeman who ticketed me was there. He testified. Then I said I was already into the intersection when the light turned.

The judge said, "case dismissed." I met my father in the hallway. He was grinning from ear to ear.

Like man since time immemorial, we had wickedly and deceitfully circumvented the law. We had mocked God and His righteousness. How would my father have liked it if someone had stolen his car, but had the fix in with the judge when he went on trial? This was a question that never came up. Had we ever heard of the Commandment, "thou shalt not bear false witness?" If we had, during those deliberations it was far from our minds. The Psalmist says, "thou leadest me on paths of righteousness for thy name's sake…." Amen. Righteousness, ethics in this case, cannot be divorced from God and His Holy Name. It is not merely a little breach, but an offense against God. Isn't that why Jesus taught that under the law we are all sinners? Only in and through God, through belief in his Son, can we be saved from the condemnation under the Law.

One of my father's favorite comments was that "The unions have to use force because management has control of 'reason' through power and money." He would add, moving easily from hatred of the bosses to hatred of his father, "Grandpop was a real mean guy – when he caught my brother and me stealing the Hebrew school tuition money to buy candy, he beat the — out of us." Wrong and right were not in his vocabulary. Stealing? If you got away with it, it was right. And from this contempt for stealing, it was easy for him to move to other immoral views. "every man wants to plant his seed in every woman in the world." Adultery? As with stealing, being caught was the only error. "If you don't take care of number one, who will?"

Friends, I am not writing this to judge my father. That is allotted to another greater than I, but I am holding these words up to you in all their gravity and depravity, that you may form a clearer picture of your own mind, and of the character and behavior of those you associate with. Do you find yourself nodding approval of my father's world view, or of his sayings? Do you find yourself wondering what alternative there is to such a view? Do you feel any sorrow or remorse in your soul for harboring or having harbored thoughts like these, or for being a poor example to the young? Perhaps this would be a good time for you to repeat with me the Lord's prayer:

Our Father Who art in Heaven
Hallowed be Thy name;
Thy Kingdom come
Thy will be done
On Earth
As it is
In Heaven;
Give us this day our daily bread
And forgive us our debts as we forgive our debtors;
And lead us not into temptation but deliver us from evil:
For thine is the Kingdom, and the Power, and the Glory
Forever.
Amen.

My father boasted about being a tough guy. "I showed up at my brother's wedding wearing dark glasses. I had gotten into a fight that afternoon with two Italian guys. I was sweeping up outside the grocery store and one of them called me a dirty —." I could not let him get away with it." On another occasion when the rabbi insisted on meeting with me when I decided to quit Hebrew school, my father said, "If the rabbi lays a hand on you, I'll go over there and beat him to a pulp." He was a tough guy, he said, yet when he lay in the hospital after a couple of heart attacks, he was in terror of dying.

He had numerous extra-marital affairs over the 25 years he was married to my mother.

For my sixteenth birthday, my father took me to a strip show at the Troc Burlesque house on Arch Street.

"Are you ready to go Eddie?" my father asked. He had been looking forward to giving me my sixteenth birthday present for weeks.

"The two of you are going to have a fine time tonight," my mother chimed in, laughing.

"I checked the papers, and the headliner is Anne 'BangBang' Arbor – sounds pretty wild," my father said with a big grin on his face.

"What do they do down there?" I asked.

"The strippers take off their clothes and dance around. The comedians tell some jokes. It's not all that wild, but every red-blooded American boy should go."

"They do bumps and grinds," my mother chimed in, "like Gypsy Rose Lee did a couple of times on the Jack Parr show a few weeks ago, remember? Bump bump-de-bump, bump-de-bump bump-de-bump."

I remembered the show with Gypsy Rose Lee, but somehow I knew this would be different. Gypsy

Rose Lee had her clothes on, but the girls at the Troc did not. I was worried. How would I react? Would I be nervous? I did not want my father to think I was a sissy.

It was my sixteenth birthday present. Going to the Troc was his way of initiating me into manhood. To him, the bar mitzvah was "just religion," but when it came to manhood, the Troc was "the real thing." (A year later he offered to fix me up with a prostitute and ridiculed me when I showed I was afraid.) After the Troc, I could begin to be bad. I think he believed that with my initiation I could begin to follow the sleazy low road of sin that was being travelled by him. And this is indeed what happened. Going to the Troc was my first giant step into the gutter. I can tell you from first hand experience that whoever says there is no danger to the minds and spirits of society from pornography, from sex jokes and sensuality on TV and in advertisements, etc. etc. is a liar!

My lustful appetites were whetted and my hunger and thirst for righteousness was blunted in a significant way by that laughing foray into filth with my father. I still imagined myself a normal boy going towards marriage, kids, and a wholesome life. I had no idea that I was being primed, trained, and steered towards a life of corruption and degradation. Innocently, albeit with a certain diabolic glee (a chip off the old block), I walked down the cement steps in front of our house.

"Have a good time," my mother waved and called as we get into the Chrysler. "Don't worry, we will," my father called back. He gave a big wink, and we climbed into the family car grinning from ear to ear.

Going to the Troc was part of my father's egotistic delusion about his grandeur as a man. Womankind is there for male pleasure, he believed. Womankind serves; man commands. Fidelity and the biblical injunction to cleave together as one flesh meant nothing to him. He denied God and His Holy Word. He was sensuous and power mad, and his goal was that I would become the same as he. But for the grace of God, but for Messiah Jesus, I would today be a prime candidate for hell or else languishing in the torment of eternal fire.

Please do not fix on my father as an individual. For in these pages, and in my mind, he represents a certain mind of sin, one to which I was attached, and one which, in my attachment, I loved and admired and desired to emulate. And even today traces of these manias and sins must be fought in my heart and mind through prayer and the seeking of God's face. Surely this mind of sin is infected with an eternal affliction. I cannot compromise with nor coddle this mind.

Oh woe, woe to those who read these pages, but do not feel the pangs of remorse eating at your hearts, who do not reflect on these grave matters. For it is not God's wish that any should perish, but rather, he calls all to belief in His son and through Him to everlasting life. As you read on, let your heart be rent, just as the people of old tore their clothes in mourning and repentance before God. May your heart be stung, and may you desire to walk closely and passionately with God from whose living spirit you have been kept (or kept yourself) separate for too long. Give up those trysts in the motels! Give up your wheedling and conniving, or outright taking and giving of bribes. Give up your contempt for the things of God, and allow yourself to regret the endless blasphemies which have come out of your mouth or to which you silently assented when they spewed forth from others. O child of God Most High, turn to your Savior today and rest with me, even now, in anticipation of our eternal and sweeter rest in Heaven.

I urge you to seek the blessings of salvation, the assurance of Heaven, and to open yourself to the grace of reconciliation with your Maker, whose blood was shed once for all 2000 years ago for forgiveness of our sins. Repent and turn to Him as your Lord and Savior.

Chapter Eight:

Will Power Was My Number One Fault

I keep praising a saving God. My life and soul have been redeemed by Jesus Christ. When Jesus died on the Cross, he uttered the words, "It is finished," before finally expiring. By that he meant the entire work of redemption for a lost and fallen humanity was completed. The prophecies of Isaiah, especially in Chapter 53 of his great prophetic writings, were fulfilled. No longer would humankind be lost in a sea of uncertainty about its relationship to a loving God. No longer would any person (me) have to wonder if heaven would be his eternal resting place. No longer would Jews have to pick their way through an infinite complexity of rules and regulations. Mercy, forgiveness, and justice would take us through to ultimate victory because of who Christ is.

Christ has finished the greatest work. Yet, my father's number one criticism of me was that I was not a finisher. He told me so many times that I was a quitter. He said, "I bought you a chemistry set after you begged me and nagged me for it, but after a little while, you got bored with it, and stopped using it." He reminded me that I had quit Hebrew school about six months after my bar mitzvah, after

having gone for 3½ years. He reminded me that I
had quit playing the violin after playing it for about
three years. When I began high school, after one
term of falling grades, I wanted to quit and go to an
easier school (I had elected to go to Central High,
a selective high school in Philadelphia). "You are
always a quitter," he said, "but you're not going to
quit this time. No matter what, you are going to go
through this school."

Had I not accomplished my bar mitzvah? Was that
not finishing? Wasn't it really my father who had quit
any affiliation with the synagogue and most things
Jewish? How could I be faulted in the face of his
disparagement of Judaism? What about his dictum,
"Do as I say, not as I do." This alone would have
been good reason for quitting. Quitting made me an
obedient son.

Had I not made a special paste with my
chemistry set that successfully prevented ice from
forming on the windows of the family car? Did my
father ask me how I did it? Did he thank me? I
don't remember so. I do remember my mother
constantly worrying out loud that I might blow
up the house. When I volunteered to do my
experiments in the basement, I was told it was too
cold and drafty down there. When you are young,
and nobody around you seems to take an interest,
and your every move is a cause for worry, then you
will quit.

And how could I find hope to continue with the
violin when my father had no interest in hearing me

practice my scratchings of the bow across the strings? My uncle, a great violinist with the Philadelphia Orchestra, had told my father than I didn't have much talent, and as far as playing the violin that was tantamount to a judgment from God.

Yet, in the matter of my continuing at my great high school, my father's insistence was not just words. He became involved. He worked with me on my compositions for English. We labored over them *together*. I stayed up late at night with him fretting and fuming at his perfectionism; yet feeling that this was really what I needed. "Logical order," he continuously stressed. "One thought has to follow from another. Then you have development and unity." The final products were a mix of his writing and mine. Were the compositions mine? In a technical sense, they were not. At the same time, I was learning what to do. His mind, his sense of the written word, was getting into my mind. I was learning. By the end of 10th grade, I was able to write successful compositions by myself. I achieved A's on my own. I had learned what to do.

Yet, my father continued to want credit for my achievements.

After a dismal 10th grade, I reveled in my successes in school. Yet, in the midst of my family, I felt like a nobody. My older brother, Myron, who was in medical school while I was in high school, had been an excellent student and athlete. My achievements were dwarfed by his. Also, my father never tired of insisting that he was the smartest bus driver who ever lived.

I had to fight my way into family conversations. I demanded year after year that I be granted more respect from my father and my brother. Inwardly, I insisted to the point of obsession, "I am worthy; I AM worthy; I am WORTHY!"

One day, my high school administered a surprise essay test to all the juniors. William Bennett had released a report on writing in America's schools that concluded the country was in a sorry state. Students could not read and they could not write. An objective observer landing from another planet might conclude that students could not think. What would the citizens of tomorrow be like? Would the Presidents of the future be cavorting mindlessly in the Oval Office? Would TV audiences be giggling at the problems of others on TV shows for psychological voyeurs? Would people someday chat in short, incoherent bursts of phrases rather than sentences? It was a horrible image of an amoral and illiterate society that disturbed the nation. The essay was an attempt to counteract that trend.

All the juniors were asked to write about the poem, "Richard Cory." Richard Cory was a fine appearing man. He was a good-looking chap, and a fine dresser. He seemed upright and happy. He seemed to be a man of means, a man of decency – someone who was in control of his life and destiny – someone to be admired and envied. Yet, one day he put a bullet through his brains.

The riveting ending and the contrasts of the poem totally intrigued me. "What a remarkable gap there is between appearance and reality, between seeming and being," I thought. I had already begun to think of myself as on a path of philosophy, and the poem touched the essence of my motivation. I wrote with a gusto and inspiration that was unusual even for a zealous student. I expanded and expounded. I dug deep into my own feelings and introspections. "We are such mysteries to ourselves," I thought. "Life is such darkness."

The junior papers were reviewed by a team of English teachers headed by Mr. Barsky. In Mr. Barsky's classes, every written piece was evaluated in light of forty-three critical points of punctuation, grammar, and rhetoric. No one's work could emerge unscathed from the probing criticism of Mr. Barsky's determined scan.

Yet, a week after the essay was turned in, Mr. Barsky called me aside in the hallway outside the English   office.

"Jeffrey, I want to tell you something."

"Yes, Mr. Barsky."

"The essay you wrote about 'Richard Cory'….it was truly remarkable, beyond anything I might have expected or imagined. It was the best essay in the entire junior class! I just want to congratulate you for that superlative effort. I don't know when I've read a student paper like that!"

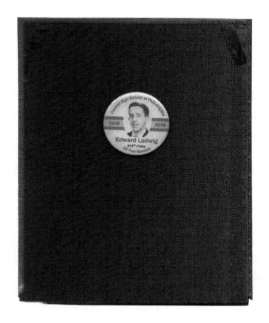

JL, Age 16, High School Senior,

I began to levitate. I floated into algebra. I floated through gym. I floated through American history (I was vaguely aware of Mr. Katz [whose thick lower lip was like my grandfather's] asking fervently, insistently, "What is *persona non grata?*... is this the same as 'diplomat without portfolio'?"). Still air borne, I boarded the subway after school.

Small, invisible wings of joy grew spontaneously between my shoulder blades, and I flew through the door. My father and older brother were seated in the living room having their usual heated discussion about whether humanity could be reduced to biological functions.

"I can't wait to tell you what happened today," I interrupted. "I wrote the best paper in the junior class on the class-wide essay "Richard Cory." It was a special test to see if the students were failing in writing, to see if our school was collapsing the way Dr. Bennett said schools were collapsing throughout the country."

"Is that so?" Myron said, grinning his broad, superior smile. "Richard Cory?" he asked. "Why that's the same poem Dad and I were discussing last month, don't you remember?" I shook my head. I did not recall any such discussion.

"Maybe I wasn't here when you were talking about it," I offered.

"Sure you were," Myron asserted. "We were talking about...."

"Well, whatever was said then, I wrote that Richard Cory had locked up his suffering inside, and that the world, living as it does in appearances, assumed and assumed and assumed about what he felt and what he thought, obsessed only with how he *appeared*. People see what they want to see. They do not want to get inside a person, or even consider that there is an inside because that would imply there was an entire sphere of experience they knew nothing about. People love to talk about behavior and appearances rather than admitting that feelings come first. Despite a world of evidence to the contrary, people want to live in appearance and express "shock" when their so-called knowledge proves false…. That's just one of the points I made in the essay."

"Jeff," Myron said, dripping with superiority, "that's just what Dad and I were saying last month…. Dad, aren't I right? Don't you remember us covering just that point?" Ellis smiled the same confident, self-satisfied smile that had appeared first on Myron's face. He took a puff of his Marlborough, and assured me that they had covered just that point, using almost the same words in their analysis of Richard Cory the previous month.

I felt crushed by their disdain. I had floated into the room, but suddenly it seemed that a bullet had bored a hole in the balloon of spirit that had carried me aloft. Determined to put on a good face, I grinned and defiantly asserted that I was taking credit for the essay, that I had written the essay, and that I deserved the praise. Although I wanted to appear untouched by their mockery, deep inside I was wounded.

Like Richard Cory, my outward determination to "claim the victory" belied my inner condition of frustration, anger, disappointment, and sense of helplessness. They wanted to make me a carbon copy, but I wanted to be an original, a success.

I made up my mind that someday they would have to acknowledge me as an equal, as a smart somebody-type person to be appreciated, and even consulted about the deep questions of life.

Chapter Nine:

A Student With The Smartest Boys in Town

W hen I entered Central High School at Ogontz & Olney Avenues in Philadelphia, I was in 10th grade, and unprepared for the demands of that competitive environment. It was the top public high school in the city. It stood in solid gray stone glory at the top of a hill, symbolic of high learning and high achievement. Only the most gifted students were admitted. While there were some good students in my junior high, over 85% of the students were rampaging through their early pubescence. Even in the 1950's, they were going wild in the junior highs, and especially the black students seemed totally out of control. The white students could not understand how they got that way. Even the wild Italian kids seemed calm and relaxed compared to the black students. Central would be another world.

Central began in ninth grade, but because of my mother's fears about my riding in the subways at such a young age (I was a year younger than my peers), I began in the tenth grade.

JL's Parents 1960

French was the only subject in which it seemed I was competitive owing to the dedicated tutoring of my French teacher who remained after school two or three days a week so I could learn various tenses of the language that were not required in my junior high curriculum. Although I have forgotten her name, I have not forgotten her kindness, and bless her now and forever for her caring, loving, motherly, giving ways.

In English class, a subject I considered my best, I was stunned by Mr. Barsky's requirements. He handed out a list of 42 items of grammar and style that he looked for in every composition. For the first time, I began receiving C's for my essays. Night after night I slaved away with my father trying to get inside the writing process and find out what I had been doing wrong. My father focused constantly on the unity of my writing – trying to get every thought to follow every preceding thought in an orderly, logical, and consistent manner, as well as on using transitional words and phrases.

My dad had had writing aspirations as a young man. Although he only had had an eighth grade education, he prided himself for being self-taught in many areas, and for his writing skills. He was always asked by the other bus drivers to write up their accident reports, and on some occasions when he was a union official, he would present arbitration cases before the arbitrator, usually an attorney or labor professor from a local university. They often complimented him in their decisions for his forceful and logical presentations, and for the paperwork that was largely written by him.

Not only was I having problems with writing, but I felt totally overshadowed by the brilliant answers of some of the other students. Sheldon in particular seemed to be someone who knew everything. No matter what question Mr. Barsky posed from the reading or respecting our general knowledge, Sheldon seemed to know the answer. If someone else should also know the answer, Sheldon always had a better way of phrasing that answer or some additional crucial point to make. When the student next to me saw the incredulous look on my face, he nudged me and said, "His father's a congressman," as though that explained everything.

Since I had just arrived, and most of the students had already been together for over a year, I asked other students in the class about Sheldon.

"Is he the smartest student in the tenth grade?"

"Sheldon? No. He's pretty good, but there's an advanced class of students, and the top of that class is way smarter than Sheldon."

"Who's that?"

"Gilbert…he's the smartest one in the tenth grade."

I couldn't imagine anyone being so smart as to even eclipse Sheldon. Would I ever meet Gilbert? Would I ever have a class with Gilbert? I was convinced that I was now in the midst of the smartest people on the face of the earth.

Every day at lunch we rushed to the cafeteria. I always brought my lunch in a brown paper bag, and only sometimes would buy something from the food counter. I always sat at the exact same table in the same seat. I can imagine it now slightly to the left of the main steam tables, but forward – the first row of tables beyond the aluminum posts separating the food dispensation area from the eating area.

Every lunch period for years, I sat with the same boys. Although we chattered away in an animated manner, we never exchanged names. We were not prep school boys who were trained in the social amenities such as introducing oneself to another. We just ate and talked.

The fellow on my left was a pleasant, soft-spoken student who wore glasses with light colored frames.

He was thin like me although a bit more fit, and his hair was cut short, almost a crew cut. It seemed to me that his head was small. The curvature of his skull was round whereas my cranium seemed to stick out in the back and my forehead was high in the top front.

We talked to each other and to others. Every topic under the sun came up. We were curious and often knowledgeable about so many social, scientific, political, philosophical, and artistic ideas.

Only after a year did I learn that the schoolmate with the small head was Gilbert.

I was proud that I had been able to get along so well with the smartest guy in the class – that I had not felt myself to be outclassed and inadequate in our daily conversations.

At Central I first heard about the Dead Sea Scrolls from Charles Lupsa in my home room while we were sitting on the floor in the hallway during a civil defense drill. At that time, there was fear of atomic attack by the Soviet Union, and we practiced going to the hallway and getting down on the floor as part of our defense [sic]. Also, Mike Luskin, the class jokester, told us about Leonard Bernstein, his mother's first cousin, who had lived with them for a long time when he was a student or teaching (I never got it straight) at Curtis School of Music. I was thrilled to think I was riding the subway with a close relative of such a famous person.

Even on the subways to and from school, especially after school, the animated discussions continued. Our schoolwork was always on our minds as were all ideas. The only time we stopped our adolescent intellectuality machine was when the girls from Most Blessed Sacrament HS boarded the subway. They immediately began rolling down their knee socks or taking those socks entirely off (right on the subway!) and began applying make-up to their beautiful sexy faces.

School, politics, and high culture were all out the window. These were fabulous nymphets who absorbed our entire attention. Sometimes they would hop off the train and light up cigarettes on the subway platforms. That was illegal, but in our eyes they were hardly felons. No...they were in a most desirable category...the category of BAD GIRLS.

I remained obsessed with the smartness of Gilbert. How could anyone be that smart?!

When we were in the same French class in 12th grade, on one occasion, the teacher asked him to turn his chair around and help teach the class. On another occasion, he answered the impossible question: what are the two dots over a letter called? We all knew that in German it is an *umlaut*, but none of us knew what an *umlaut* is called in English. Only Gilbert knew.

One day I went to the Guidance Counselor and asked him to tell me Gilbert's IQ and my IQ.

"Why do you want to know?" he asked.

"I just thought it would be interesting," I replied.

"Well, Jeffrey, I'm not allowed to tell you that information. At any rate, if you'd like to know, stop back tomorrow, but I really can't tell you."

The next day I returned to my Guidance Counselor's office. Mr. Zuckerberg was nowhere in sight, although his door was open. I paced around outside for about ten minutes waiting for him. Then, somehow or someone, prompted me to go inside his office.

Lying on his desk was a small slip of white paper. On the paper was Gilbert's name and a number, and my name and a number underneath. My number was expressed in a range, from/to. For Gilbert there was one number.

Gilbert's number was six points higher than the highest number in my range.

———

I fought against the idea that there was an unbridgeable gap between Gilbert's abilities and mine.

As seniors, the French Prize Exam was held for all students who wished to compete. Eight of us showed up. Each of us was given a number so that the teachers would not know whose paper they were grading.

I was number six, but I was inwardly grousing that Gilbert was assigned number one. If I knew he was number one, surely the teachers grading the exams would know he was number one. What was the point of the so-called coding?

It seemed to me that if he were having a bad day, and I were having an exceptionally good day, I might edge him out for the prize. It never occurred to me that any of the other six might be better than I, only Gilbert.

Gilbert won the Prize. Second and Third Prizes were not selected.

Chapter Ten:

SUCCESS AT ANY PRICE

Through my years of high school, I was motivated and controlled by fantasies of status, self-indulgence, running things, people deferring to me, and having lots of money to pursue my erotic fantasies. Lascivious and power mad, I frequently had the dream of flying a la superman, and swooping down almost like a bird of prey to kidnap various women and take them back to a secret cave where they would have to indulge my every whim. My nights were often spent "in the cave," and my daylight hours were spent in the dog eat dog jungle of a public high school for gifted boys. Our studies were our obsession. Every examination was an intense moment of trust. To me, even the one point difference between an 89 and a 90 was almost a matter of life and death. I would chew angrily for days on end, whipping myself for missing the 90, and on one occasion angrily disputed with a teacher who refused to give me the A- I was sure I deserved.

The test results were compared among the students with unbelievable competitive zeal. How Noel mocked me one day when he received a French test score three points higher than mine. And how proud, even smug, I felt when my grades surpassed those of my best friend, Harold. When we had a social studies class together, I recall trying hard not to gloat as I bested him in test after test. Knowing how pride always desires that we see ourselves in the best light, I am certain that I gloated openly much more than I succeeded in suppressing said gloating.

In fact, after high school, Harold and I went to different colleges, and I often wondered at how abruptly our friendship ended. The fact that we chose different career paths and had gone to different schools did not seem to be sufficient explanation for the total rift. We still remained in the same city, and did not live far from each other.

It strikes me now that the real reason for our rift was my gloating and sense of superiority over my better grades, my hubris. I did not intend to gloat; yet undoubtedly assumed an arrogant attitude towards my friend. How strange, ironic, and sad that in the Christian era, after 2000 years of learning the importance of the inner man, that I and so many others have become very ignorant of the behavior of the outer man. So much is justified in terms of the good intentions of people and by the assumption that it is the realization of the inner man only that is important. Often Christians and non-Christians will fall into this trap. What is the net effect of these misassumptions and lack of awareness of the moral, psychological, and spiritual implications of our BEHAVIOR? The net effect, I believe, is that the Ten Commandments are more relevant than ever before. The outer man and woman must be balanced with that inner man and with the demands of Almighty God for a life of repentance, prayer, humility, and goodness.

How delighted I am today to be able to proclaim myself to be a man, a Jewish man, who has been born again, who follows and believes in Jesus Christ! How satisfying it is to know that the full gospel – the Hebrew Scriptures and the New Testament – express the whole truth of God, and that the old is not replaced by the new, but the new is a fulfillment of the old, perfecting the old, perfecting the prophecies of the Messiah, and enlarging unto salvation itself our understanding of *tanakh* (the Hebrew Scriptures). I see it as part of Divine Providence and Mercy that the entire vista of the Holy Bible opens before me. From this vantage point, great opportunities and revelations are open which were hid since before the foundations of the world.

With me, the put down system, the competitive system, was a way of life. In school and at home, one-upsmanship was the key. In this climate, I built a loser psychology. Pride was our God. If I put down others, I would lose friends and feel rejected. If I did not put down others, I would feel put down, and feel as though I were a "loser" in the struggle in life for supremacy.

The sense of being a loser in the dialogues at home between and among my father, brother, and me infected my attitudes in the competitive world at school. Even when it seemed I had a victory, I doubted myself, and felt that the so-called victory was but a prelude to a defeat. I always felt I was barely holding on. How thrilled and happy I was when I first heard the words of Jesus the Christ saying,

"What greater love has any man than this that he lay down his life for his friends." That truth seemed to express the exact opposite of what I experienced at home with my father and brother. It seemed to me that they were saying to me that we lived in a world of survival of the fittest and that if anyone had to survive it would be they, for their greater gifts would live on. But Jesus taught me something different. Life does not end at death. Our experience of this world is not definitive. Rather, life is eternal, and we can spend it with Him joyfully achieving eternal victory.

2012: From left: Wife Zeny; Sister-in-law, Nene; Daughter, Hannah; JL (2012)

Made in the USA
Charleston, SC
28 August 2013